Learn CSS In One Day and Learn It Well

CSS for Beginners with Hands-On Project

The only book you need to start coding in CSS immediately

http://www.learncodingfast.com/css

Preface

This book is written to help you learn CSS FAST and learn it WELL.

The book does not assume any prior background in coding. If you are an absolute beginner, you'll find that this book explains complex concepts in an easy to understand manner. If you are an experienced coder but new to CSS, this book will provide you with enough depth to start coding in CSS immediately.

All examples and images in the book are carefully chosen to demonstrate each concept so that you can gain a deeper understand of the language. Each CSS chapter also comes with an exercise at the end of the chapter. The exercises are designed to help you further strengthen your understanding. The source code for all the exercises can be found in the appendix at the end of the book.

In addition, as Richard Branson puts it: "The best way of learning about anything is by doing". This book comes with an additional bonus project where you'll be guided through the coding of a webpage entirely from scratch. The project uses concepts covered in the book and gives you a chance to see how it all ties together.

You can download the bonus project and the source code for all the exercises at http://www.learncodingfast.com/css.

Contact Information

I would love to hear from you.
For feedback or queries, you can contact me at
jamie@learncodingfast.com.

More Books by Jamie

Python: Learn Python in One Day and Learn It Well

Table Of Contents

Chapter 1: Introduction 8
  Tools of the Trade 8
  Opening a .HTML File..9

Chapter 2: Basics of HTML 11
  What is HTML..11
  Basic Structure of a HTML Page 12
    Doctype 13
    Start and End Tags...13
    The Head Element 14
    The Body Element 14
  Elements Within the Head Element 15
  Elements Within the Body Element................................20
    Elements for Adding Content to the Page 20
    Elements Used in Conjunction with CSS.......................24
    Elements For Adding Javascript Code to Website 26
    Elements For Formatting Text.....................................26
    Elements for Defining Sections of a Webpage 27
  Comments 29
  Character Entities 30

Chapter 3: Basics of CSS 32
  Applying CSS Code...33
  Syntax of a CSS rule..35
  Selecting an Element 36
    Selecting Classes and IDs 36
    More Selectors 40
  Case Insensitivity 44
  Order of Precedence 45
  Display Inconsistency 48
  Comments 50
  Exercise 3 50

Exercise 3.1 51

Chapter 4: CSS Box Model 56
What is the CSS Box Model 56
Width and Height Properties 59
Overflow Property 60
Padding and Margin Properties 61
Border Properties 63
border-width 63
border-color 64
border-style 65
border-radius 66
Border Shorthand 67
Exercise 4 67
Exercise 4.1 67

Chapter 5: Positioning and Floating 73
Positioning 73
Static Positioning 73
Relative Positioning 74
Fixed Positioning 77
Absolute Positioning 77
Floating 79
Exercise 5 84
Exercise 5.1 84
Exercise 5.2 87

Chapter 6: Display and Visibility 89
Display 89
Visibility 90
Exercise 6 91
Exercise 6.1 91

Chapter 7: Background 93
 Background Color 93
 Background Image 93
  background-image 94
  background-repeat 94
  background-attachment 95
  background-position.. 95
 Exercise 7 97
  Exercise 7.1 97

Chapter 8: Text and Font 100
 Font Properties 100
  font-family 100
  font-size 101
  font-style 103
  font-weight 103
 Text Properties 104
  color 104
  text-alignment 104
  text-decoration 105
  letter-spacing 105
  word-spacing 106
  line-height 106
 Exercise 8 107
  Exercise 8.1 107

Chapter 9: Lists, Links and Navigation Bars 111
 CSS Lists.. 111
  list-style-type 111
  list-style-image 112
  list-style-position 113
  list-style 114
 CSS Links 114
 Navigation Bars 116

Exercise 9 117
   Exercise 9.1 118
   Exercise 9.2 119

Chapter 10: Tables 121
Border, Padding and Margin 121
Height and Width 123
Text Alignment 125
Background, Font and Text 125
nth-child( ) Selector 126
Exercise 10 126
   Exercise 10.1 127

Bonus Project 131

Thank You 132

Appendix A: Source Code for Exercises 133

Chapter 1: Introduction

Welcome to the world of CSS. I am so glad and honoured that you picked up this book. Before we embark on this learning journey together, let us first define what is CSS.

CSS stands for Cascading Stylesheet and is used for the styling and design of a website. It is one of the many languages a web programmer uses to create a website. Other web languages include HTML, Javascript and PHP, just to name a few.

HTML is concerned with the content and structure of a website. As a website's existence is meaningless without content, knowing HTML is essential for anyone interested in web programming. This book will first start with an introduction to HTML, covering some of the essential basics you need to know about HTML. While this coverage is by no means comprehensive, it should be enough for you to perform most of the HTML tasks necessary. If you are familiar with HTML, feel free to skip to Chapter 3.

Tools of the Trade

Before we start coding our HTML and CSS pages, let us first look at some of the recommended tools for doing web programming.

At the most basic level, you only need a web browser (e.g. Internet Explorer, Chrome, Safari, Firefox) and a text editor (e.g. Notepad) to start coding websites. However, unless you belong to the school of thought that real programmers shouldn't use any programming aid, I strongly encourage you to use some of the free tools available online to make your coding life easier.

One of the most recommended tool is an advanced text editor that offers syntax highlighting. Syntax highlighting means the editor will display text in different colors depending on the purpose of the text. For instance, the editor may use red color for keywords, blue for comments and green for variables. This simple feature will make your code much easier to read and debug. If you are on a Windows machine, I suggest Notepad++ (http://notepad-plus-plus.org/). For Mac, I suggest TextWrangler (http://www.barebones.com/products/textwrangler/). Both are free to use.

Opening a .HTML File

An .HTML file can be opened in two ways. One way is to open it in a web browser by double clicking on the file. This is for viewing the page. Another way is to open it in a text-editor for editing. To do that, first launch your text-editor and then open the file from within the editor.

When working with HTML files, I suggest you open the file in your browser and text-editor concurrently and arrange the two windows so that they are side-by-side. That way, you can edit the code on your editor, save it, and then move over to your browser, refresh the page and immediately check the effects of the changes you made to the code. Follow this procedure when working on the exercises from Chapters 3 to 10.

Chapter 2: Basics of HTML

Now that we've covered a basic introduction to web programming, let's start learning some actual HTML code. In this chapter, we'll be covering the essentials of HTML. If you are familiar with HTML, you can skip the chapter and go ahead to Chapter 3.

For those of you who are new to HTML, let's get started.

What is HTML

HTML stands for Hypertext Markup Language and is a language used by web programmers to add content to a web page. A markup language is simply a language for annotating a document to explain what different sections of the text are and how they should be presented. For instance, we can use HTML to specify whether the content should be presented as a list or in table form. The current HTML version is HTML5.

The nicest thing about HTML is that the source code of a web page is free for all to view. This makes it easy for us to learn HTML by studying the codes of other web pages. To view the source code of a web page on Windows, simply right-click anywhere on the page and select "View Source" (or something similar, such as "View Page Source", depending on the browser you use). If you are on Mac, click on "View" in the menu bar, select "Developer" and then select "View Source".

Most of the source code that you view will look very complicated, especially if you have no prior knowledge in HTML. Don't worry about that. Soon, you'll be able to write such 'complicated' codes yourself.

To get a better understanding of how HTML5 works, let's start by examining the basic structure of a HTML document.

Basic Structure of a HTML Page

An example of a basic HTML document is shown below. I've added numbers beside each line of the code for easy reference. These numbers are not part of the actual code.

```
1   <!doctype html>
2   <html>
3   <head>
4       <title>My First HTML Page</title>
5   </head>
6   <body>
7       <p>This is just text</p>
8       <img src="someimage.jpg" alt="Just some
image">
9   </body>
10  </html>
```

As you can see from the code above, HTML uses a lot of angle brackets with a single word enclosed inside, such as <head> and <body>. These are known as tags and each tag has a specific meaning in HTML.

Doctype

On line 1, the `<!doctype html>` tag tells the browser that this document uses HTML5. If you check the source of older web pages, you may see something like `<!DOCTYPE HTML PUBLIC "-//W3C//DTD HTML 4.01//EN" "http://www.w3.org/TR/html4/strict.dtd">`. This means they are using other versions of HTML, such as HTML4.01 in this case.

Start and End Tags

On line 2, the `<html>` tag tells the browser that the actual HTML code starts here. Most tags in HTML have a corresponding end tag. The end tag for the `<html>` tag is found on line 10. It has an additional forward slash (/) before the word `html`.

Note that not all tags in HTML have end tags. For instance, the `<img>` tag, which is used to add images to our webpage does not have an end tag. Generally, there is a need for an end tag when we need to let the browser know where the effect of the tag should end. For instance, if we want to bold some text in HTML, we can write

```
This text is <strong>important</strong>, but
this text is not.
```

We'll get

This text is **important**, but this text is not.

The `<strong>` tag and the `</strong>` tag tells the browser where the bold effect should start and where it should end. In contrast, there is no need to tell the browser where an inserted image should end. Hence, the `<img>` tag does not require an end tag.

The Head Element

On line 3, we have the start of the `head` element.

In the broadest sense, a HTML document is made up of two main elements, the `head` and the `body` elements.

The `head` element provides general information about the document, including its meta data, title and links to additional resources. It starts with the `<head>` tag on line 3 and ends with the `</head>` tag on line 5. Within the `<head>`...`</head>` tags, we enclose other tags that provide all these behind-the-scene information about the document.

In our example, we only included information about the title in our `head` element. The `title` element (on line 4) shows the title that the browser should display on its title bar or on the page's tab. In this case, the text "My First HTML Page" will be displayed. We'll cover more tags that are used within the `head` element in a later section.

The Body Element

Line 6 is where the `body` element starts. Contents within the `<body>`...`</body>` tags will be displayed on the webpage. In our example, the text "This is just text" and the image "someimage.jpg" will be displayed.

There are a lot of other tags that we can use inside the `<body>`...`</body>` tags, such as the `<img>` tag for adding images, the `<table>` tag for displaying tables and the `<ul>` tag for adding a list. We'll cover these tags in detail later.

To get a feel of how this works, you can download the code for this chapter from the accompanying website (http://learncodingfast.com/css). The source code can be found in the *Chapter 2 - Basics of HTML* folder. Double click on the HTML file to launch it.

You will also be guided through the coding of an actual HTML document when working on the bonus project that comes with this book. The source code for the project can be found in the *Bonus Project\Answers* folder.

Elements Within the Head Element

Now that we understand how HTML works, let us look at the `head` element in detail.

As mentioned above, the `head` element provides general information about the document, such as its metadata, title and links to external resources. Let's look at some of the tags within the `head` element.

<u><meta></u>

The `<meta>` tag is included within the `<head>`...`</head>` tags and is used to provide additional information about the website to the browser, search engines or other web services. These information will not be displayed on the page itself. The `<meta>` tag does not have an end tag.

One common use of the `<meta>` tag is to provide keywords for search engines. An example is:

```
<meta name="keywords" content="HTML, CSS, Learn
in One Day">
```

You may notice that this tag is a lot longer than the tags we discussed earlier. This is because the `<meta>` tag has two attributes, `name` and `content`.

`name` is used to specify the type of information the tag contains (keywords in this case), while `content` is used to specify the content of the information.

You can also give a description of your website using the `name=description` attribute. An example is:

```
<meta name="description" content="This is my
first Website. It teaches you how to use HTML
and CSS">
```

Another common use of the `<meta>` tag is to use it to specify how the browser should control the page zoom level and dimensions. This is done using the `name=viewport` attribute. For instance, you can write

```
<meta name="viewport" content="width=300,
initial-scale=1">
```

`width=300` sets the width of the viewport to be equals to 300 pixels. One pixel, px, is equal to one dot on the computer screen.

When you set the viewport to 300px and you have an image that is, say, 500 pixels wide, you will only see a portion of the image as the image's width is larger than the width of the viewport. To see the rest of the image, you have to scroll the page. In contrast, if you set the viewport to 500px, the entire image will be shown without any scrolling needed. If you set the viewport to 1000px, the entire image will be shown too, but it'll be smaller and occupy only half the width of the screen.

`initial-scale=1` sets the initial zoom level (1x in this case) of the page when it is first loaded by the browser.

If you are interested in finding out more about how the viewport works, you can check out https://developer.apple.com/library/ios/documentation/Appl eApplications/Reference/SafariWebContent/UsingtheView port/UsingtheViewport.html

<title>...</title>

The `<title>` tag is used for defining the title that the browser should display on its title bar or on the page's tab.

<style>...</style>

The `<style>` tag is used to add internal CSS code to our HTML document. We'll learn how to do that in Chapter 3.

Example:
```
<style type="text/css">
body {
    ...
}
</style>
```

<link>

The `<link>` tag is used to link to an external resource, most commonly used to link to an external CSS stylesheet. It does not require an end tag.

Example:
```
<link rel="stylesheet" type="text/css"
href="mystyle.css">
```

The `rel` and `type` attributes simply tell the browser that you are linking to a CSS stylesheet. You do not need to modify them. The only attribute that you need to modify is the `href` attribute. This attribute is used to state the path of the CSS file.

How to Write Paths to External Files

The path of any external file always starts from the current folder of the HTML document. Suppose we have five folders: 'User', 'Documents', 'MyWebsite', 'MyCSS' and 'MoreCSS' with the following structure:

User > Documents > MyWebsite > MyCSS > MoreCSS

That is, the 'User' folder contains the 'Documents' folder, which in turn contains the 'MyWebsite' folder. Within the 'MyWesbite' folder, we have the 'MyCSS' folder, which contains the 'MoreCSS' folder.

If you are working on a HTML file in 'MyWebsite' and you want to link to 'mystyle.css' in the SAME folder, you simply write `href = "mystyle.css"`.

However, if 'mystyle.css' is in the 'MyCSS' folder (one level down), you have to write `href = "MyCSS/mystyle.css"`. If it is in 'MoreCSS' (two levels down), you have to write

`href = "MyCSS/MoreCSS/mystyle.css"`

If 'mystyle.css' is in the 'Documents' folder (one level up), you have to use ../ to move one level up. You write `href = "../mystyle.css"`. If it is in the 'User' folder, you have to move two levels up. You write `href = "../../mystyle.css"`.

Elements Within the Body Element

Now that we've covered the elements within the `head` element, let us move on to the `body` element.

Elements for Adding Content to the Page

First, let us discuss some commonly used elements for adding content to our webpage. These tags are enclosed within the `<body>...</body>` tags.

<u>\<p>... \</p></u>

This is the paragraph tag and is used to add text to a page. Any content within the two tags will be displayed as a paragraph. By default, most browsers will add a line before and after a paragraph.

Example:
```
<p>This is a paragraph</p>
```

<u>\<img></u>

This `<img>` tag is for adding images to your webpage. It requires you to provide some additional information like the location of the image, its height and width etc. Commonly used attributes of the `<img>` tag include:

`src:`
Stands for "source" and is used to state the path of the image. The `src` attribute must be provided.

`height:`

For specifying the desired display height of the image

`width:`

For specifying the desired display width of the image

`alt:`

Stands for "alternate" and is used to specify the text to display if the image fails to load.

Example:
```
<img src="images/myImage.jpg" height="100px" width="100px" alt="My Image">
```

This will insert the image "myImage.jpg" onto the webpage. The image will be scaled to a size of 100px by 100px. If the image fails to load, the text "My Image" will be displayed instead.

<u>\<a>...\</a></u>

The `<a>` tag is used to insert a hyperlink. The most important attribute for the `<a>` tag is `href` which is used to specify the URL of the page the link goes to.

Example:
```
<a href="http://www.google.com">Click here to
go to Google</a>
```

Output:
<u>Click here to go to Google</u>

Clicking on the link will bring you to the Google website.

<u>\<h1\>...\</h1\> to \<h6\>...\</h6\></u>

The \<h1\> to \<h6\> tags are heading tags and are used to define HTML headings. \<h1\> is the most important heading and \<h6\> is the least important. Text within heading tags are normally displayed with a larger font size on the browser, with h1 having the largest font size and h6 having the smallest.

Example:
```
<h1>This is the most important heading.</h1>
<h2>This is the second most important
heading.</h2>
```

Output:

This is the most important heading.
This is the second most important heading.

<u>\<ol\>...\</ol\> and \<li\>...\</li\></u>

The \<ol\> tag stands for ordered list and is used to create a list with numbers or alphabets as list markers.

Example:
```
<ol>
  <li>Chocolate</li>
  <li>Strawberry</li>
  <li>Vanilla</li>
</ol>
```

Output:
1. Chocolate
2. Strawberry
3. Vanilla

<ul>...</ul> and <li>...</li>

The `<ul>` tag stands for unordered list and is similar to the `<ol>` tag. However, instead of using numbers or alphabets as list markers, it uses shapes (such as a dot, or a hollow circle).

<table>...</table>, <tr>...</tr>, <th>...<th>, <td>...</td>

The `<table>` tag is used to create a table. `<tr>` stands for "Table Row", `<th>` stands for "Table Header" and `<td>` stands for "Table Data". Tables are created row by row in HTML.

Example (numbers are not part of the code):

```
1   <table>
2     <tr>
3       <th>Name</th>
4       <th>Gender</th>
5     </tr>
6     <tr>
7       <td>Abigail</td>
8       <td>F</td>
9     </tr>
10    <tr>
11      <td>Benny</td>
12      <td>M</td>
13    </tr>
14  </table>
```

This code will give you a table with 3 rows and 2 columns. Line 2 to 5 defines the first row of the table, which is a header row as the `<th>` tag is used. Line 6 to 9 defines the second row and lines 10 to 13 defines the third. Depending on how you style the table in CSS, you'll get a table similar to the one below:

Name	Gender
Abigail	F
Benny	M

Elements Used in Conjunction with CSS

There are two special HTML elements that do not have any inherent meaning in HTML. They are mainly used in conjunction with CSS to style a specific section of the webpage. These two elements are `div` and `span`.

<ins><div>...</div></ins>

`<div>` stands for 'division' and is used to define a division or a section in a HTML document. The `<div>` tag is normally used in conjunction with CSS to format the contents within the `<div>...</div>` tags.

For instance, if we write

```
<div>
     This is some division in the HTML
document.
     <ol>
```

```
        <li>Chocolate</li>
        <li>Strawberry</li>
        <li>Vanilla</li>
    </ol>
</div>
```

we can use CSS to format everything inside the `div` tags (i.e. both the text and the ordered list). We'll learn how to do that in the next chapter.

...

The `<span>` tag is similar to the `<div>` tag. The main difference is that `<div>` is a block element, while `<span>` is an inline element.

A block element is one that starts and ends with a new line break. In contrast, an inline element does not start or end with a line break. For instance, if we write

```
This is a <div>block element</div>, while this
is an <span>inline</span> element.
```

we'll get

```
This is a
block element
, while this is an inline element.
```

As the phrase 'block element' is tagged with the `<div>` tag, it starts and ends on a new line. On the other hand, the word 'inline' is an inline element and does not start or end on a new line. Generally, we tend to use `<div>` to wrap sections of a document, while `<span>` is used to wrap small portions of text, images, etc

Elements For Adding Javascript Code to Website

<u>`<script>`...`</script>`</u>

The `<script>` tag is used to add internal Javascript code to our HTML document or to link to an external script. Javascript is a scripting language that adds interactivity to our website.

Example (to add internal JS code):
```
<script>
document.getElementById("para1").innerHTML =
"Hello JavaScript!";
</script>
```

Example (to link to an external JS script):
```
<script type="text/javascript"
src="myscripts.js"></script>
```

Elements For Formatting Text

<u>`<strong>`...`</strong>`</u>

The `<strong>` tag is used to define important text. Most browsers will bold the text.

Example:
```
The examination will be held on <strong>12 Jan
```

```
at 2pm</strong>. Latecomers will not be allowed
into the hall.
```

Output:

The examination will be held on **12 Jan at 2pm**. Latecomers
will not be allowed into the hall.

<u>\<em\>...\</em\></u>

The `<em>` tag is used to define emphasized text. Most
browsers will display the text in italics form.

Example:
```
The examination will be held on 12 Jan at 2pm.
Latecomers <em>will not</em> be allowed into
the hall.
```

Output:

The examination will be held on 12 Jan at 2pm. Latecomers
will not be allowed into the hall.

Elements for Defining Sections of a Webpage

HTML also comes with a few tags for defining sections of
a webpage. These tags do not do much, their purpose is
simply to indicate to the browser and developer which
section the content they enclose belongs to.

<u>\<header\>...\</header\></u>

The `header` element defines the top section of a webpage
and normally consists of the logo/banner of the website. Do

not confuse the header element with the head element. The head element defines all the behind the scene stuff and is not displayed on the page. The header element on the other hand defines content that is to be displayed at the top of the website.

<nav>...</nav>

nav stands for navigation and is used to define a set of navigation links (i.e. menu).

<main>...</main>

The main element is used to define the main section of a page.

<footer>...</footer>

The footer element is the counterpart of the header element and is used to define the footer of the web page (i.e. the bottom section). The header and footer elements are similar to the 'header' and 'footer' sections of a MS Word document. For Word documents, we normally use the footer to display the page number. On a website, we normally use it to include additional links and additional information (such as contact information and copyright information).

Note that all the four elements above are to be included in the <body>...</body>. Their purpose is mainly to further segment the `<body>` element into different sections. The code below shows how these elements are used.

```
<!doctype html>
<html>
<head><title>An example</titlte></head>
<body>
    <header>
    <!-- Insert Banner or Logo Here -->
    </header>
    <nav>
    <!-- Insert Navigation Links Here -->
    </nav>
    <main>
    <!-- Insert Main Content Here -->
    </main>
    <footer>
    <!-- Insert Footer Here -->
    </footer>
</body>
</html>
```

Comments

Notice that in the previous example, we used a lot of the `<!--` and `-->` symbols? These are known as comments.

Most of the time when we program, we need to add comments to our code to make it easier to read and understand. This is extremely important if we are working with other programmers or if we need to edit the source code at a later date. Comments are not displayed in the browser, they are merely added to explain our code.

To add comments to a HTML documents, we use the `<!--`
`... -->` tag.

Example:
```
<!--This is a comment. It will not be displayed
in the browser.-->
```

Character Entities

Some characters have predefined meanings in HTML and are reserved for that specific use. For instance, the less than sign (<) is used to start all tags. What happens if we need to display the text 5<12 on our webpage?

To do that, we need to use character entities. Character entities always start with an ampersand sign (&) and end with a semi-colon (;). There are two ways to display the less than sign. We can either write `&lt;` or `&#60;`. The first is known as the entity name while the latter is known as the entity number. An entity name is easier to remember (`lt` stands for less than) but some browsers do not support all entity names. On the other hand, entity numbers are harder to remember but the support is better.

Commonly used character entities include

Less than sign (<)
`&lt;` or `&#60;`

Greater than sign (>)
`&gt;` or `&#62;`

Ampersand sign (&)

`&amp;` or `&#38;`

For instance, if you want to display 5<12 on your website, you write it as `5&lt;12` in your HTML code.

Another commonly used character entity is non-breaking space (` `). A non breaking space entity is used to display consecutive spaces. By default, HTML does not recognise consecutive spaces. If you write 5 spaces in your HTML code, the browser will remove 4 of them and display only one space. For instance, if you write

`"There are 5 spaces     here"`

the browser will display it as

`"There are 5 spaces here"`.

If you want to display more than one space, you need to write

`"There are 5 spaces`
`    here"`.

Chapter 3: Basics of CSS

Now that we've covered quite a bit of HTML, let's move on to CSS. CSS stands for Cascading Stylesheet and as the name suggests, CSS is all about styling and making your website look gorgeous.

The latest version of CSS is CSS3. Unlike previous versions of CSS (namely CSS1 and CSS2.1), CSS3 splits the language into different modules so that each module can be developed separately at a different pace. Each module adds new features or extends the capabilities of features previously defined in CSS 2.1. Essentially, CSS3 is simply an extension of CSS2.1.

This book covers the core properties of CSS2.1 as well as a few new properties that are introduced in CSS3. Once you master the core properties, you will have no problems moving on to more advanced properties that are newly added in CSS3. These advanced properties allow for more fanciful styling of your website, such as adding transitions and animations.

In this chapter, we'll be covering the basics of CSS, including its syntax and order of precedence. However, before going into the syntax of CSS, let's first learn how to add CSS rules to our web site.

Applying CSS Code

There are three ways to apply CSS code to our site.

The first is by linking to an external file. This is the recommended method. To do linking, you need to write your CSS rules in a separate text file and save it with a .css extension. The syntax for adding the rules to your HTML code is

```
<link rel="stylesheet" type="text/css" href="style.css">
```

You add the <link> tag to the head element, between the <head>...</head> tags. The first two attributes rel and type tell the browser that this is a CSS stylesheet. You do not need to modify them. The last attribute href is where you specify the path to the CSS file that you want to link to. A CSS file is simply a file that contains CSS rules, without any HTML tags. An example is shown below. Don't worry if the code does not make sense to you, we'll cover them very soon.

```
body {
    margin: 0;
    background-color: green;
}
```

Save this code as "style.css" in the same folder as the .html file. You can then use the <link> tag above to link this CSS file to your HTML file.

The second method to add CSS rules to our site is to embed the code directly into our HTML source code, within the head element. This is done with the `<style>` tag. An example is shown below. The embedded CSS code starts after the `<style>` start tag and ends before the `</style>` end tag.

```
<head>
     <style>
     div {
            color: blue;
            width: 100px;
            height: 200px;
     }
     </style>
</head>
```

The last method is to use inline CSS. Inline CSS is specified in the start tag of the element you want to apply it to, using the `style` attribute. Each rule ends with a semi-colon (;). An example is:

```
<div style="text-decoration:underline;
color:blue;">Some text</div>
```

Out of the three methods, linking is the preferred method. Linking separates the HTML content from the styling rules and makes it easier to maintain our codes. It is also extremely useful when we need to apply the same CSS rules to multiple web pages.

Embedded CSS, on the other hand, is commonly used when the rules only apply to one web page.

Inline CSS is handy when you need to apply a rule to only one element, or when you want to override other CSS rules that apply to the same element. This is because inline CSS has a higher precedence than CSS code added using the other two methods. We'll discuss order of precedence later in this chapter. However, inline CSS mixes styling with content and should be avoided whenever possible.

Syntax of a CSS rule

Now that we know how to apply CSS rules to our HTML files, let's move on to learn some actual CSS code. The first thing to learn about CSS is its syntax, which is relatively straightforward. The syntax is:

```
selector { property : value; property : value;
property : value; }
```

For instance, if you want to style the contents inside a `<div>` tag, you write the rule as

```
div {
  background-color: green;
  font-size: 12px;
}
```

The first word `div` is the selector. It tells the browser that the set of rules inside the curly brackets { } applies to all elements with the `<div>` tag.

Inside the curly brackets, you write all your declarations. You start by declaring the property that you want to set (`background-color` in the first declaration), followed by a colon (:). Next, you give the value that you want (`green` in this case). Finally, you end each declaration with a semi-colon (;).

Indentation and line breaks do not matter in CSS. You can also write your declarations like this:

```
div { background-color: green; font-size: 12px;
     }
```

Pretty straightforward right? Great! Let's move on...

Selecting an Element

In the example above, the rules declared in the curly brackets will apply to ALL elements with a `<div>` tag. However, most of the time, we want greater variation. Suppose you want one `<div>` element to have a font size of 12px and another to have a font size of 14px. How would you do it?

Selecting Classes and IDs

There are basically two ways to do it. The first method is to use the `id` attribute. In your HTML document, instead of just using the `<div>` tag, you can add an `id` attribute to it. For instance, you can write

```
<div id="para1">
     Some text.
```

```
</div>

<div id="para2">
      More text.
</div>
```

In our CSS code, we can then select the respective id by adding a # sign in front of the id name. An example is shown below:

```
div {
   background-color: green;
}

#para1
{
   font-size: 12px;
}

#para2
{
   font-size: 14px;
}
```

The first rule applies to all elements with the <div> tag. The second rule only applies to the element with id="para1". The third rule only applies to the element with id="para2".

In addition to using the selector #para1, you can also be more specific and write div#para1, with no space before and after the # sign. Both methods will select the same element, but the second method has a higher precedence (more on this later).

Note that an `id` should be unique within a page. Two `<div id="para1">` tags is not allowed. One `<div id="para1">` and one `<p id="para1">` tag is also not allowed as both have the same `id`. Although your HTML and CSS code will work even if you have two elements with the same `id`, problems will arise when you start using Javascript or other scripting languages on your website.

If you need to apply the same CSS rules to two different elements, you can use a `class`. A `class` is similar to an `id`, with the exception that a `class` need not be unique. In addition, an `id` has a higher precedence than a `class`.

For now, let's consider the following code:

```
<div class="myclass1">
     Some text.
</div>

<p class="myclass1">
     More text.
</p>

<div>
     Yet more text.
</div>
```

If you want to select all `<div>` elements (i.e. the first and third element), you write

```
div { … }
```

If you want to select all elements with `class="myclass1"` (i.e. the first and second element), you add a dot (.) in front of the `class` name, like this:

```
.myclass1 { … }
```

If you only want to select `<p>` tags with `class="myclass1"` (i.e. the second element), you write

```
p.myclass { … }
```

There should be no space before and after the dot.

An element can have more than one classes. Multiple classes are separated with a space in the HTML attribute. For instance, the `div` below has two classes: `myclass1` and `myclass2`.

```
<div class="myclass1 myclass2">
…
</div>
```

If we have the following CSS code,

```
.myclass1 { … }

.myclass2 { … }
```

the rules for both `myclass1` and `myclass2` will apply to the above `<div>`.

More Selectors

In addition to selecting an element by `id` and `class`, CSS offers a large variety of ways to specify the elements that we want to select.

Selecting Multiple Elements

For instance, we can select multiple elements at one go. If we want to select the `<div>`, `<p>` and `<ul>` elements, we write:

```
div, p, ul { … }
```

Selecting Child Elements

If we want to select all the `<p>` elements *inside* `<div>` elements, we write

```
div p { … }
```

Note that there is no comma between `div` and `p`. In this case, the CSS rules will only apply to `<p>` elements that are inside `<div>` elements. For instance, if we have the HTML structure below, the rules will apply to `I am a paragraph inside div` and not to `I am a stand-alone paragraph`.

```
<div>
     <p>I am a paragraph inside div</p>
</div>

<p>I am a stand-alone paragraph</p>
```

The first paragraph 'I am a paragraph inside div' is called a child element of the `<div>` tag as its start and end tags (`<p>` and `</p>`) lie entirely within the `<div>...</div>` tags.

Selecting by Attribute

You can also select an element based on its attribute. If you want to select all hyperlinks that link to http://www.learncodingfast.com, you write

```
a[href="http://www.learncodingfast.com"]  { … }
```

There should be no space before the square bracket. If you have the following HTML code, only the first link will be selected.

```
<a href="http://www.learncodingfast.com">Learn
Coding Fast</a>
<a href="http://www.google.com">Google</a>
```

Selecting Pseudo-classes

Another commonly used selector is the pseudo-class selector. A pseudo-class refers to a *special state of an element*. The most common pseudo-classes are those for the `<a>...</a>` element. A hyperlink can be in one of four states:

link (an unvisited link)
visited (a visited link)

`hover` (when the user mouses over it), or
`active` (when the link is clicked).

We can select a hyperlink based on the state it is in. For instance, to select the hover state, we write

```
a:hover { … }
```

The keyword `hover` is added to the back of the `a` selector using a colon (:), with no spaces before and after the colon. We'll come back to the concept of selecting and styling different states of a hyperlink in Chapter 9.

In addition to selecting different states of a hyperlink, we can also use pseudo-classes is to select child elements. Suppose we have a `<div>` element with three `<p>` child elements:

```
<div>
    <p>I am the first child</p>
    <p>I am the second child</p>
    <p>I am the third child</p>
</div>
```

We can use the `first-child` pseudo-class to select the first `<p>` element. We can also use the `last-child` selector to select the last child or the `nth-child(n)` selector to select the nth child.

For instance, if we write

```
p:nth-child(2) { … }
```

we'll be selecting the paragraph `I am the second child'` because of the number `2'` in the parenthesis ( ).

Selecting Pseudo-elements

In addition to pseudo-classes, CSS also has the concept of pseudo-elements. A pseudo-element refers to a specified part of an element, such as the first letter or the first line of an element.

For instance, if we have the following <p> element:

```
<p>This is some text.</p>
```

We can select the first letter (T) by writing

```
p::first-letter { ... }
```

Note that a double colon is used in this case. Another pseudo-element is the `first-line` element. This will select the first line of the text.

Finally, we can use the `before` and `after` pseudo-elements to insert content before, or after, the content of an element. For instance, if we want to add an exclamation mark after all `H1` elements, we can write

```
h1::after {
      content: "!";
}
```

This will automatically append an exclamation mark after all `H1` elements. If we have the following HTML code

```
<h1>This is a heading</h1>
```

we'll get

```
This is a heading!
```

Case Insensitivity

For the most part, CSS selectors and rules are case-insensitive. Hence, you can either write

```
div {
      Background-color: GREEN;
}
```

or

```
DIV {

      background-coloR: green;
}
```

Both will work equally well. The only exception to this case-insensitivity is when selecting classes and ids.

If we have

```
<div id= "myID">Some text</div>
```

`div#myID` will select the above element while `div#MYID` will not.

Order of Precedence

Now that we've learnt how to select elements, let us move on to a very important concept in CSS: order of precedence.

As mentioned earlier, we can apply CSS code to our website in three different ways. It is common for a programmer to use more than one way to apply CSS code to a site. For instance, a website may have CSS rules defined in an external file AND some additional CSS rules embedded within its `<style>...</style>` tags. This may result in more than one rule being applied to the same element. One of the most frustrating experience about working with CSS, especially when you are first starting out, is when you try to apply a css style to an element and the page simply seems to ignore your rule. Most of the time, this is due to the order of precedence. Specifically, this happens when more than one rule applies to the same element, and another rule has a higher precedence than the one you are specifying.

Three principles control which CSS rule has a higher precedence.

Principle 1: The more specific the selector, the higher the precedence

We won't go into details about how to calculate the specificity of a selector. The main point to remember is that an `id` is considered to be more specific than a `class`, and a `class` more specific than an element. Let's consider the code below:

```
div { font-size: 10px; }
#myId { font-size: 12px; }
.myClass { font-size: 14px; }

<div id="myId" class="myClass">Some text</div>
```

Since the `<div>` element has `class="myClass"` and `id="myId"`, all three rules `div`, `#myId` and `.myClass` will apply to the `<div>` element. However, as `id` has the highest precedence, "`Some text`" will be displayed with a font size of 12px.

In addition, another point to note about specificity is that the more detailed your selector, the higher the precedence. For instance, `div#myId` has a higher precedence than `#myId`. This is because `div#myId` is considered to be more detailed as it tells us that `myId` is an `id` of the `div` element. In the sample code below, the color yellow will be applied.

```
div { color: red; }
div#myId { color: yellow; }
#myId { color: blue; }
.myClass { color: green; }

<div id="myId" class="myClass">Some text</div>
```

Principle 2: If no style is specified, elements inherit styles from their parent container

A child element is an element which lies entirely within the start and end tags of another element. For instance, in the code below, `<p>` is a child element of the `<body>` element. Since the font size of `<p>` is not defined, it'll inherit this property from the `<body>` element for which the property is defined.

```
body {
      font-size: 1.5em;
}

<body>
      <p>Some text</p>
</body>
```

If the `font-size` property is also not defined for the `<body>` element, the browser's default font size will be used.

Principle 3: All else being equal, the last declared rule wins

Suppose you have the following CSS declaration in your HTML `<head>` element.

```
<head>
<style>
      p { font-size: 20px; }
</style>
</head>
```

Further down the HTML document, you have the following HTML code, with an inline CSS rule:

```
<p style="font-size: 30px;">Some text</p>
```

Which rule do you think will be applied to the words "Some text"?

The correct answer is the inline rule. This is because all things being equal, the rule that is declared last has the highest precedence. Since inline CSS is declared within the HTML code, it is declared later than the embedded CSS which is declared in the `head` section. Hence, a font size of 30px will be applied.

Display Inconsistency

Another issue to deal with when working with CSS is the problem of display inconsistency across browsers. You may find that your website looks slightly (or drastically) different in different browsers. Most display issues tend to occur in older versions of Internet Explorer, although issues can occur in other browsers too (especially mobile browsers).

Display inconsistencies occur because different browsers use different layout engines to interpret the site's CSS code. For instance, Safari and Chrome use the WebKit engine while Firefox uses the Gecko engine. One engine may calculate and display a page differently from another engine. For instance Trident, the engine used by Internet Explorer, automatically widens a page's pixel width for certain page designs. This can lead to the sidebar being pushed to the bottom due to insufficient width.

Another problem causing display inconsistency is the lack

of universal support for some CSS properties. Some properties are not supported by all browsers. You can go to the site http://www.caniuse.com to check if a certain CSS property is supported by the browser that you are developing for.

Sometimes, a certain CSS property is supported by a particular browser only when we add a prefix to our CSS rules. This is especially true for newer properties in CSS3. An example is the `column-count` property in CSS3. This property divides an element into multiple columns. For instance, we can divide a `div` element into three columns by writing `column-count: 3`.

This property is not supported by older versions of Firefox, Chrome, Safari and Opera. To enable the property to work on these browsers, you have to write it as three declarations,

```
-webkit-column-count: 3;
-moz-column-count: 3;
column-count: 3;
```

instead of just

```
column-count: 3;
```

The `-webkit-` prefix adds support for older versions of Chrome, Safari and Opera while the `-moz-` prefix adds support for Firefox. In addition, we also have the `-ms-` prefix that adds support for Internet Explorer.

When creating your website, it is useful to test it on various browsers to ensure that nothing is broken. The way to fix a 'broken' display depends on the issue causing it. If you are really stuck, I suggest searching or posting the question on http://stackoverflow.com, which is a very useful online community for programmers.

Comments

The last thing to cover in this chapter is comments. In CSS, we add comments to our code using the /*...*/ symbols. An example is as follows:

```
/*
The rules below are comments.

p {
        background-color: black;
        font-size: 20px;
        color: white;
}
*/
```

Everything between the /* and */ symbols is ignored by the browser.

Exercise 3

Download the source code for this exercise from http://learncodingfast.com/css and unzip the file. The source code for this exercise can be found in the *Chapter 3 - Basics of CSS* folder.

Exercise 3.1

1. Open the file *Chapter 3 - Basics of CSS.html* concurrently in your browser and text editor.

2. First, look for the following lines in the source code in your text editor:

```
p {
        background-color: yellow;
}
```

This selects all the <p> elements and sets their background colors to yellow. The line 'This is some text in the div element.' is not selected because it is not within any <p>...</p> tags.

3. Now let's try changing the rule from

```
p {
        background-color: yellow;
}
```

to

```
P {
        Background-coloR: YELLOW;
}
```

Save the file in your text editor and refresh your browser. Notice that nothing changes? This is because CSS is not case-sensitive in most cases.

4. Now, let us try to select different HTML elements and observe which elements end up with a yellow background. For each item below, simply change the selector on line 6 in the HTML file to the required selector.

   First, let's select the element with class = "myClassPara". To do that, change the p selector in the CSS rule to .myClassPara. Save the file in the editor and refresh the page in the browser. Notice which paragraph is selected now.

5. Now change the selector to .myclasspara. Notice that nothing is selected now? That is because CSS is case-sensitive when selecting classes and ids.

6. Next, let's select the element with id = "myIDPara". Try doing it yourself.

   Got it? You can change .myClassPara to either p#myIDPara or just #myIDPara. Notice which paragraph is selected.
   Try changing #myIDPara to #MYIDPARA. Notice that nothing is selected?

7. Next, let's learn how to select more than one elements. Try selecting both the h1 and h2 elements.

   The way to do it is simply to change the selector to h1, h2.

8. Next try selecting the `div` element.

   To do it, simply change the selector to `div`.

9. Now, let's select the `p` element inside the `div` element. To do this, we write `div p` as the selector. Notice which elements are selected.

10. Next, try selecting all the link (`<a>`) elements.

    What do you notice? The links are now highlighted in yellow right?

11. Next, we'll narrow down our selection based on HTML attributes. Try selecting the link with `href="http://www.learncodingfast.com"`. The correct way to do this is with square brackets as follows:

    `a[href="http://www.learncodingfast.com"]`

    Try it. Only the first link will have a yellow background now.

12. Next, we'll use the pseudo-class selector to change the background color of all link elements when we hover over them. Try changing

    `a[href="http://www.learncodingfast.com"]`

    to

```
a:hover
```

Save the file and refresh the browser. Notice that nothing is selected? Now hover your mouse over any of the hyperlinks and observe what happens.

13. Next, let's try to select the second child element of the div element. You do that by changing the selector to

```
p:nth-child(2)
```

14. Now, let's try selecting the first letter of all <p> elements. You use the pseudo-element first-letter to do that. Change the selector to

```
p::first-letter
```

15. Next, let's look at what happens when an element has more than one classes. Change the selector back to .myClassPara and add the following CSS code just before the </style> tag.

```
.mySecondClassPara {
    text-decoration: underline;
}
```

Notice which paragraph is both yellow in background AND underlined. This is because that paragraph has two classes: myClassPara and mySecondClassPara. Therefore, both rules apply to it.

16. Finally, let's try adding an exclamation mark to the end of all <p> elements. We'll use the after pseudo-

element to do that. Add the following CSS code just before the `</style>` tag.

```
p::after{
    content: "!";
}
```

Chapter 4: CSS Box Model

So far, we've covered the basics of HTML and CSS. In this chapter, we'll start to do some actual CSS coding. Specifically, we'll learn about the CSS box model and look at how we can modify the look and feel of a box in CSS.

What is the CSS Box Model

All elements in CSS are treated as boxes. CSS boxes consist of margins, borders, padding, and the actual content as shown below.

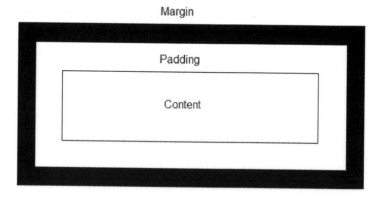

The thick black line is the border. Within the border is the padding and the actual content. Outside the border is the margin of the box. The thickness of the padding, border and margin can all be modified with CSS. To understand how this box model works, let's analyze the code below. You can download this code at http://learncodingfast.com/css.

```
<!doctype html>
<html>
<head><title>Chapter 4 - CSS Box Model</title>

<style type="text/css">

#box1 {
     margin: 20px;
     padding: 10px;
     border: 5px solid black;
     width: 100px;
     height: 100px;
     text-align: justify;
     float: left;
}

#box2 {
     margin: 20px;
     padding: 50px;
     border: 5px solid black;
     width: 100px;
     height: 100px;
     text-align: justify;
     float: left;
}
</style></head>

<body>
<div id="box1">Learn CSS in One Day and Learn
It Well. CSS is easy.</div>
<div id="box2">Learn CSS in One Day and Learn
It Well. CSS is easy.</div>

<p>skajd fhadlc vkas j cnl ka jshvn aclaks
jdclkasjd ckasj cnkas djvcn ksa mc nlkasd jn
skajd fhadlc vkas j cnl ka jshvn aclaks
jdclkasjd ckasj cnkas djvcn ksa mc nlkasd jn
skajd fhadlc vkas j cnl ka jshvn aclaks
```

```
jdclkasjd ckasj cnkas djvcn ksa mc nlkasd
jn</p>
</body>
</html>
```

If you run this code, you'll get the boxes below. The gibberish text beside and below the boxes is added to show the margin.

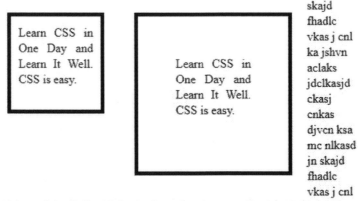

skajd fhadlc vkas j cnl ka jshvn aclaks jdclkasjd ckasj cnkas djvcn ksa mc nlkasd jn skajd fhadlc vkas j cnl ka jshvn aclaks jdclkasjd ckasj cnkas djvcn ksa mc nlkasd jn

This code defines two boxes with width and height of 100 pixels. This width and height refers to the dimensions of the **content area only**.

The first box (box1) has a padding of 10 pixels (px) around the content area. Around the padding, it has a solid black border of 5px. The total width of box1 **(including its border)** is 100 (content area) +10*2 (padding on both sides) +5*2 (border on both sides) = 130 px. The same applies for the height.

The second box (box2) has a padding of 50px. Despite box2 being much larger than box1, notice that the text "Learn CSS in One Day and Learn It Well. CSS is easy." still occupies the same area? This is because the content area is determined by the width and height properties, not by the padding. box2 has a total width of 100+50*2+5*2 = 210px. Its height is also 210px.

Outside the border, we have a margin of 20px for both boxes. Notice there some space between the gibberish text and the boxes? That is the margin.

Try playing around with the code a bit and changing the values of the width, height, padding, margin and border properties. Observe what is affected by each change. You should notice that width and height affects the content area. Margin affects the area outside the border while padding affects the area inside. Border is of course the border of the box. We'll cover each of these properties in detail next.

Width and Height Properties

The width and height properties of a CSS box specify the dimensions of the content area (excluding the padding, border and margin). The values are normally given in pixels or as a percentage. For instance, the code in our example sets the width and height of both box1 and box2 to 100px. You can also set the width to 80%. The boxes' content area will then occupy 80% of the width of the page. Finally, you can set the height and width to auto. In this case, the browser will calculate these values automatically, based on the amount of space needed to display the content inside the box.

Overflow Property

Sometimes, the width and height of the content area may be too small to accommodate the contents inside the box. By default the content will flow out of the box and overlap other contents. This results in a very badly formatted web page. If you do not want this to happen, you can use the `overflow` property. The diagram below shows how content is displayed using different values for the `overflow` property (`visible`, `hidden`, `scroll` and `auto`).

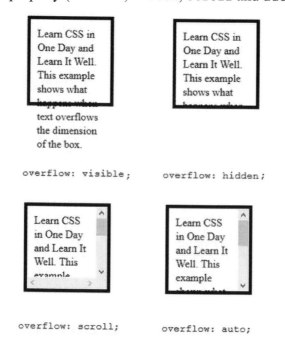

Padding and Margin Properties

Paddings and margins are both transparent. Hence we cannot change their color. However, we can specify their width. The most commonly used unit for specifying width is the pixel. If you want the margin to be 10 pixels, you write `margin: 10px;`. There should not be any space between 10 and px.

The examples below show four different syntaxes for specifying margin width. The same works for paddings. Just change the property name from `margin` to `padding`.

Syntax 1
```
margin: 25px;
```

This syntax sets all four margins to 25px.

Syntax 2
```
margin: 25px 50px;
```

This syntax sets the top and bottom margins to 25px; the left and right margins to 50px.

Syntax 3
```
margin-top: 25px;
margin-right: 50px;
margin-bottom: 60px;
margin-left: 10px;
```

This syntax sets the individual margins separately.

<u>Syntax 4</u>
```
margin: 25px 50px 60px 10px;
```

This syntax is a shorthand for syntax 3. The four numbers specify the values of the individual margins, starting from the top and continuing in a clockwise direction. Hence top margin is 25px; right is 50px, bottom 60px and left 10px.

In addition to having positive values, margins can have negative values. A negative margin will result in overlapping or hidden content. For instance, if we change the margin of box2 from `margin: 20px;` to `margin: 20px 20px 20px -50px;` (i.e. `margin-left` is changed to -50px), we'll get the following:

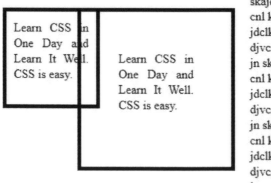

Note that while margins can have negative values, paddings cannot have negative values.

Margins are also commonly used to align block elements. By default, block elements take up the full width available. However, you can change this width using the `width` property. For instance, the code below changes the width of an element to 80%. You can then center align the element by setting the left and right margins to auto.

```
width: 80%;
margin: 0 auto;
```

The `margin` rule above sets the top and bottom margins to 0px (the unit px is optional if the value is 0) and the left and right margins to auto. When margins are set to auto, the browser will evenly distribute the remaining width to the left and right margin, resulting in a center aligned element.

Border Properties

CSS `border` properties allow you to set the width, color, style and radius of an element's border.

border-width

To set the thickness of the border, you use the `border-width` property. Border width is normally set in pixels. Alternatively, you can use one of three predefined values: `thin`, `medium` or `thick`. Border properties are set using the same syntaxes as margins and paddings.

Examples:

```
border-width: 25px;
```
will set all borders to 25px.

```
border-width: 25px thin;
```
will set the top and bottom width to 25px and the left and right width to thin.

```
border-top-width: 30px;
```
will set the top border to 30px.

border-color

To set border color, you use the property `border-color`. The value of this property can be set by specifying a predefined color name, such as `green`, `red` and `yellow` etc. A total of 140 such names are defined in CSS. The site http://www.w3schools.com/cssref/css_colornames.asp gives a complete list of these names. In addition, you can also set the color to transparent, by writing `border-color: transparent;`.

Another method to specify border color is to use the RGB notation (e.g. `rgb(0,255,0)`). All web colors are represented by three primary colors: Red, Green and Blue. If you write `rgb(0, 255, 0)`, it means you want the second color (i.e. green) to have an intensity of 255 (the maximum intensity), and the first and third colors (red and blue respectively) to have an intensity of 0 (the least). This will simply give you the color green.

In addition to using the RGB notation, you can also use the hexadecimal notation, which uses 6 digits to represent color. The first two numbers represent the hexadecimal value for the intensity of 'red', the next two represent 'green' and the last two represent 'blue'. Often a color tool is used to generate these hexadecimal values. Check out the site http://instant-eyedropper.com/ for one such free tool.

Alternatively, you can go to http://html-color-codes.info/ where there's a color chart for you to select the color that you want. Click on it and you'll be given the corresponding hexadecimal value.

Examples:

```
border-color: rgb(255, 0, 0);
```
will set all borders to red.

```
border-color: red green;
```
will set the top and bottom borders to red and the left and right borders to green.

```
border-top-color: #12005F;
```
will set the top border to #12005F.

border-style

To set border style, you use the property `border-style`. The acceptable values are: `none`, `dotted`, `dashed`, `solid`, `double`, `groove`, `ridge`, `inset` and `outset`. For instance, if you write

```
border-style: solid dotted;
```

the top and bottom border will be solid while the left and

right will be dotted. If you want to set the style individually, you can write

```
border-top-style: solid;
border-left-style: dotted;
```

border-radius

The `border-radius` property is used to create borders with rounded corners. The value is normally given in pixel or percentage.

Border radius can be set individually for the four corners. The four corners are `top-left`, `top-right`, `bottom-right` and `bottom-left`.

Examples:

```
border-radius: 5px;
```
sets the border radii of all corners to 5px.

```
border-radius: 10px 20px;
```
sets the top-left and bottom-right (i.e. the two corners diagonally opposite each other) radii to 10px and the top-right and bottom-left radii to 20px.

```
border-radius: 25px 5px 0 50px;
```
sets the values of the individual corners, starting from the top-left corner and continuing in a clockwise direction.

```
border-top-left-radius: 10px;
```
sets the top-left border radius to 10px.

If the element has width and height of 100px, padding of 20px and border width of 50 px (total width and total height = 100 + 20*2 + 50*2 = 240px), setting the border radius to 120px (240 divided by 2) will give you a circle instead of a square.

Border Shorthand

The `border` property is a shorthand for specifying border width, style and color in one line, instead of doing it separately. Simply write

```
border: 5px solid green;
```

The values are for width (5px), style (solid) and color (green) respectively. Border radius is not included in this shorthand.

Exercise 4

Download the source code for this exercise from http://learncodingfast.com/css and unzip the file. The source code for this exercise can be found in the *Chapter 4 - CSS Box Model* folder.

Exercise 4.1

1. Open the file *Chapter 4 - CSS Box Model.html* concurrently in your browser and text editor.

2. Resize your browser window and observe how the gibberish text flows around the bigger box.

3. Modify the CSS declaration for `box1` by changing `width: 100px;` and `height: 100px;` to each of the following:

   (a) `width: 200px; height: 200px;`
   (b) `width: 60%;`
   (c) `height: auto; width: auto;`

   Save the file in the text editor and refresh the page in the browser. Notice what happens to `box1` in each case.

4. Now change the width and height of `box1` back to 100px and change the text between the tags `<div id="box1">...</div>` to:

   "Learn CSS in One Day and Learn It Well. This example shows what happens when text overflows the dimension of the box."

   Next, add each of the following to the CSS declaration of `box1` and notice what happens in each case:

   (a) `overflow: visible;`
   (b) `overflow: hidden;`
   (c) `overflow: scroll;`
   (d) `overflow: auto;`

5. Modify the CSS declaration for `box1` by changing `margin: 20px;` to each of the following and notice what happens to the space around `box1` in each case:

(a) `margin: 50px;`
(b) `margin: -50px;`
(c) `margin: 25px 200px;`
(d) `margin: 25px 50px 60px 10px;`

6. Remove the margin rules for `box1` and add the 4 lines below:

```
margin-top: 25px;
margin-right: 50px;
margin-bottom: 60px;
margin-left: 10px;
```

Notice any changes to `box1`? There should be no change as this is the same as 5(d) above.

7. Remove the margin rules for `box1` and add the line below:

```
margin: 0 auto;
```

Next, change the width of `box1` to 80%. Finally, remove the line `float: left;`. Notice what happens. (We'll explain what `float` does in the next chapter). `box1` is now center-aligned.

8. Now, let's work on `box2`. Modify the CSS declaration for `box2` by changing `padding: 50px;` to each of the

following and notice what happens inside `box2`.

(a) `padding: 25px;`
(b) `padding: -10px;` (refer to note below)
(c) `padding: 25px 50px;`
(d) `padding: 25px 50px 60px 10px;`

8(b) will not work as paddings cannot have negative values. You'll just end up with a padding of 0 pixel.

9. Remove the padding rules for `box2` and add the 4 lines below:

```
padding-top: 25px;
padding-right: 50px;
padding-bottom: 60px;
padding-left: 10px;
```

Notice any changes to `box2`? There should be no change as this is the same as 8(d) above.

10. Now let's change the border style for `box2`. Remove the line `border: 5px solid black;` from the CSS declaration of `box2` and add each of the following. Notice what happens to the border in each case:

(a) `border-style: solid dotted;`
(b) `border-style: none dashed double groove;`
(c) `border-style: inset;`
(d) `border-style: outset;`

11. Next, remove the `border-style` rule for `box2` and add the following:

```
border-top-style: dotted;
border-left-style: double;
```

12. Now remove the rules from part 11 and change border style to solid (`border-style: solid;`)

    Next add each of the following rules. Notice what happens to `box2` in each case.

    (a) `border-width: 25px;`
    (b) `border-width: 25px thin;`
    (c) `border-top-width: 30px;`

13. Now we are going to change the border color for `box2`. Try adding each of the following rules:

    (a) `border-color: rgb(255, 0, 0);`
    (b) `border-color: red green;`
    (c) `border-top-color: #12FF5F;`

14. Next, we'll try the border shorthand. Remove all the border properties for `box2`. Add the following:

```
border: 5px solid green;
```

15. Now, let's try the `border-radius` property. Try each of the following:

    (a) `border-radius: 20px;`

(b) `border-radius: 10px 20px;`

(c) `border-radius: 25px 5px 0 50px;`

(d) `border-top-left-radius: 10px;`

16. Finally, let's try to create a circle. First, change the width and height of `box2` to 100px, padding to 20px and the property

```
border: 5px solid green;
```

to

```
border: 50px solid green;.
```

Now, remove all previous rules for border radius and add the following rule:

```
border-radius: 120px;
```

You end up with a circle right? That's because the border radius is half of the total height (and width) of `box2`.

Chapter 5: Positioning and Floating

Now that we understand the CSS box model, let's look at how to use CSS to specify the arrangement of these boxes on our web pages. In this chapter, we'll be looking at two of the most important concepts in CSS: positioning and floating. Together, these two properties handle the layout of our web pages.

Positioning

The CSS positioning property allows you to position an element and specify which element should be on top in case of an overlap.

There are four methods to position an element. To understand how the four methods work, I strongly encourage you to try out the exercise at the end of this chapter. This is a topic that is difficult to understand without a hands-on approach.

Static Positioning

The first positioning method is `static` positioning. Static doesn't mean much, it just means that the elements are positioned according to the normal flow of the page. All HTML elements are positioned using this method by default. If you want to specify that `static` positioning be used (for instance to override another positioning rule for the same element), you write

```
position: static;
```

Relative Positioning

The second method to position an element is the `relative` positioning method. This method positions an element <u>relative to its normal position</u>. Normal position refers to the default position of the element when no positioning rule is specified or when `static` positioning is used.

Suppose we have two boxes, `box1` and `box2` with no positioning specified. If we create `box2` after `box1` in our HTML code, `box2` will be positioned below `box1` by default (refer to code below).

```
<!DOCTYPE html>
<html>
<head>
<style>

#box1 {
      /*Some rules for styling box1*/
}

#box2 {
      /*Some rules for styling box2*/
}
</style>
</head>

<body>
```

```
<div id="box1">Box 1</div>
<div id="box2">Box 2</div>
</body>
</html>
```

Now suppose we add the following rules to the CSS declaration of box2.

```
position: relative;
left: 150px;
top: 50px;
```

What we've done is change the positioning of box2 to relative positioning.

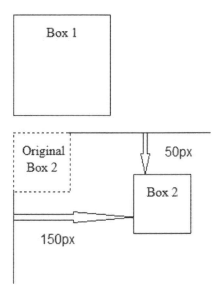

The image above shows the position of box2 when relative positioning is used. A white dotted box is added to show the original position of box2.

When `relative` positioning is applied, `box2` is moved relative to its <u>normal</u> position. The line `top: 50px;` moves the box 50px away from the top of the original position and the line `left: 150px;` moves it 150px away from the left.

You can also use the `right` and `bottom` properties to position `box2`. For instance, `bottom: 50px;` will move `box2` 50px up from the original bottom of `box2` while `right: 50px;` will move it 50px left from the original right edge of `box2`. In addition, you can use negative pixels to position the boxes (e.g. `left: -50px`)

Try the exercise for Chapter 5 and play around with the values to see how all these work.

Note that when `relative` positioning is used, the element can end up overlapping other elements.

If you want to specify which element should be in front, you have to use the `z-index` property. The `z-index` property works on any element that has a position of either `relative`, `fixed` or `absolute` (i.e. not `static`). An element with greater `z-index` value will be positioned in front of an element with a lower `z-index` value.

Suppose you have two boxes, `greenBox` and `redBox`, and they overlap each other. If you declare the `z-index` of `greenBox` as

```
z-index: 1;
```

and the `z-index` of `redBox` as
`z-index: 2;`

`redBox` will be on top of `greenBox` as it has a greater `z-index` value.

Fixed Positioning

The third positioning method is `fixed` positioning. As the name suggests, an element that is positioned using the `fixed` method will always stay at its assigned location; it will not move even when the page is scrolled. Fixed positioning is commonly used to position social sharing buttons at the side of a web page. To use `fixed` positioning, we write

`position: fixed;`

When using `fixed` positioning, we can use the `top` property to specify the number of pixels the box should be from the top of the page while the `left` property specifies the number of pixels it should be from the left of the page.

In addition to `top` and `left`, there are also the `right` and `bottom` properties, which specify the number of pixels the box should be from the right side and bottom of the page respectively.

Absolute Positioning

The final method is `absolute` positioning.

When `absolute` positioning is used, an element is positioned <u>relative to the first parent element that has a position other than static</u>. If no such element is found, it is positioned relative to the page.

For instance, suppose we have the following HTML code:

```
<div id="box1">Content in Box 1</div>
<div id="box2">Content in Box 2</div>
```

and the following CSS declaration:

```
#box1 {
      position: relative;
}

#box2 {
      position: absolute;
      top: 50px;
      left: 150px;
}
```

Assuming that `box2` is not a child element of any element that has a non static positioning, it'll be positioned relative to the page. That is, it is positioned 50px from the top of the page and 150px from the left.

However, if we change the HTML structure to

```
<div id="box1">Content in Box 1
      <div id="box2">Content in Box 2</div>
</div>
```

`box2` is now a child element of `box1`. Hence `box2` will be positioned relative to `box1`. It is now 50px down from the top and 150px right from the left side of `box1`.

In a way, `absolute` positioning is similar to `relative` positioning, except that the element is positioned relative to its parent element instead of its normal position.

Floating

The next CSS property we are going to discuss is floating.

Floating is a technique used to arrange elements on a page. The idea is similar to putting books onto a bookshelf. Imagine you have a stack of books of varying thickness and height and you need to put all the books onto a bookshelf. In addition, you are not allowed to rearrange the books. That is, the books must be placed onto the bookshelf in the same order as they were in the original stack.

To perform this task CSS-style, we'll start with the top row. We'll put the books one by one onto the top row, starting from left to right. Suppose the top row is almost full and you have a book that is too thick to fit onto the top row. What do you do? You'll move to the next row below it, right? Well, CSS does it a little differently. CSS will try to fit this 'book' onto the same row, below the previous 'book', as long as there is some space below it (refer to Box 5 in the next diagram). This method of stacking the books is similar to doing a `float: left` in CSS.

Alternatively, you can do a `float: right` in CSS. This is equivalent to starting from the top row but stacking the books from right to left.

To see how this works in CSS, suppose we have 7 `div` boxes of varying heights and widths that are floated left (refer to code below):

```
<!doctype html>
<html>
<head><title>CSS Float</title>

<style type="text/css">
div {
     padding: 10px;
     border: 1px dashed black;
     margin: 5px;
     float: left;
}

#box1 {
     width: 60px;
     height: 100px;
}
#box2 {
     width: 100px;
     height: 20px;
}

#box3 {
     width: 50px;
     height: 150px;
}
#box4 {
     width: 20px;
     height: 50px;
}
```

```
#box5 {
      width: 150px;
      height: 120px;
}
#box6 {
      width: 120px;
      height: 70px;
}
#box7 {
      width: 25px;
      height: 80px;
}

</style></head>

<body>
      <div id="box1">Box 1</div>
      <div id="box2">Box 2</div>
      <div id="box3">Box 3</div>
      <div id="box4">Box 4</div>
      <div id="box5">Box 5</div>
      <div id="box6">Box 6</div>
      <div id="box7">Box 7</div>

</body>
</html>
```

If we run this code, we'll get something like the next image.

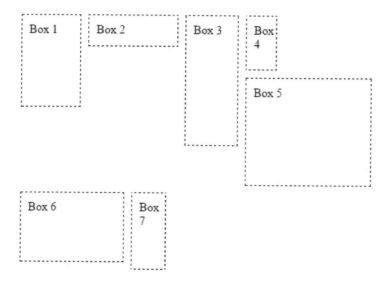

Notice how the boxes are arranged from left to right, starting from the top. As box 5 is too thick to fit into the top row, CSS places it below the previous box.

Now suppose in addition to these 7 boxes, we also have the following text that we want to display on the site.

```
<p>This is some text that is not floated.</p>
<p>This is more text that is not floated.</p>
<p>This is yet more text that is not
floated.</p>
```

If these paragraphs are included in the HTML document after the `div` boxes, we'll get the diagram below. These paragraphs will just 'squeeze' into whatever space is available.

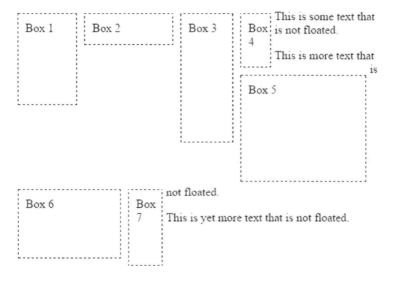

If you do not want that to happen, you can clear the float by using the `clear: both` property. To do that, make the following addition to the CSS declaration:

```
.clearFloat { clear: both; }
```

To use this class, we add it to the first `<p>` tag:

```
<p class="clearFloat">This is some text that is
not floated.</p>
```

You only need to add the `clearFloat` class to the first `<p>` tag. Once you clear the float, the text will no longer wrap around the boxes.

That's the gist of how positioning and floating works in CSS. I strongly encourage you to try the exercises for this Chapter to get a better understanding of these two concepts.

Exercise 5

Download the source code for this exercise from http://learncodingfast.com/css and unzip the file. The source code for this exercise can be found in the *Chapter 5 - Positioning and Floating* folder.

Exercise 5.1

1. Open the file *Chapter 5 - Positioning.html* concurrently in your browser and text editor.

2. Add the rule `position: static;` to the CSS declaration for `#box1` and `#box2` and observe what happens to the positions of the two boxes.

   Nothing changes right? That's because all HTML elements are positioned using `static` positioning by default.

3. Remove the rule `position: static;` from the CSS declaration for `#box1` and `#box2`. Add the following lines to the CSS declaration of #box2.

   ```
   position: relative;
   top: 50px;
   left: 70px;
   ```

   Observe what happens to the position of the second box. 3. It is now 50px from the top and 10px from the left of its normal position.

Play around with different values for the `top` and `left` properties and see what happens to the position of `box2`. Try negative values as well. You can also try using the `right` and `bottom` properties.

4. Now change the CSS declaration of #box2 back to

```
position: relative;
top: 50px;
left: 70px;
```

Notice that the text is partially hidden by the red box?

If you want the text to appear in front of the red box, add the following lines to the CSS declaration of `p`.

```
position: relative;
z-index: 2;
```

You can set the position to either `relative`, `absolute` or `fixed`. It does not matter as long as it is not `static`.

Next, add the line `z-index: 1;` to the CSS declaration of #box2. Refresh the page. The text should now be in front of the red box since the `z-index` of the text is greater than the `z-index` of the red box..

If you want the red box to be in front of the text instead, just change the `z-index` of #box2 to a value greater than 2.

5. Now, change the height of `#box1` to `5000px` and the positioning of `#box2` to `fixed` (`position: fixed;`).

   Scroll the page. 5. The red box does not move as it uses fixed positioning now.

6. Change the positioning for `#box2` back to `relative` and the height of `#box1` back to `100px`. Add the following line just before the `<p>` tag in the HTML code at the bottom of the file.

   ```
   <div id="box3"></div>
   ```

   Now add the following CSS declaration to style `box3`.

   ```
   #box3 {
       position: absolute;
       top: 50px;
       left: 150px;
       background-color: yellow;
       width: 50px;
       height: 50px;
       padding: 20px;
       border: 5px dotted black;
       margin: 10px;
   }
   ```

   `box3` uses `absolute` positioning and since it is not a child element of any `<div>` elements, it is positioned relative to the page. That is, it is positioned 50px from the top of the page and 150px from the left.

7. Now change the `<div>` code for the three boxes to the following:

```
<div id="box1"> </div>
<div id="box2">
   <div id="box3"></div>
</div>
```

box3 is now a child element of box2. Therefore it is
positioned 50px down from the top and 150px right
from the left side of box2 as it is now positioned
relative to box2.

Exercise 5.2

1. Open the file *Chapter 5 - Floating.html* concurrently in
   your browser and text editor.

2. Resize your browser-window to see what happens when
   the <div> elements do not have enough room.

3. Modify the CSS declaration for div by changing
   float: left; to float: right;. Observe what
   happens to the positions of the boxes.

4. Now change the rule back to float: left; and add
   the code below to the HTML code, just above the
   </body> tag.

```
<p>This is some text that is not
floated.</p>
<p>This is more text that is not
floated.</p>
<p>This is yet more text that is not
floated.</p>
```

Refresh the page and observe where the text is. Resize the browser window to see what happens when the width of the page is narrow.

5. Next, add the code

```
.clearFloat { clear: both; }
```

to the CSS declaration just above the `</style>` tag.

Change the first `<p>` tag to `<p class="clearFloat">` and observe what happens.

Chapter 6: Display and Visibility

Congratulations. You have now learned a fair bit of CSS. In fact, we have covered most of the important concepts in CSS, including the CSS box model and the idea of floating and positioning. In this chapter, we'll look at how to pull a disappearing act in CSS.

That's right. CSS has not one, but two, properties that allow us to remove or hide an element. These two properties are the `display` and `visibility` properties.

Display

The CSS `display` property is used to modify how an element is displayed. There are three commonly used values: `none`, `inline` and `block`.

The first value 'none' makes an element disappear. The page will be displayed as if the element is not there.

The second value 'inline' causes an element to be displayed as an inline element. We briefly talked about inline elements in Chapter 2 when discussing the difference between `<div>` and `<span>`. Recall that an inline element does not start and end with a new line. Another characteristic of an inline element is that it will only take up as much height and width as it needs. Hence, there is no point specifying the height and width of an inline element.

In contrast, a block element starts and ends with a new line and its height and width can be changed. If you want an element to be displayed as a block element, you use the 'block' value.

Example:

```
display: none;
```

Visibility

The CSS visibility property is used to hide an element. You do that by writing visibility: hidden;.

The difference between visibility: hidden and display: none is that for the former, the element is hidden but still takes up space. Using the visibility property is just like wearing an invisible cloak. The element is still there, even though you can't see it.

In contrast, when you use display: none, the element is essentially removed from the page and the page will display as if the element does not exist at all.

For instance, suppose the two properties are applied to the word "magic" in the sentence "This is just like magic. You can make words disappear." below:

For visibility: hidden; you'll get
"This is just like   . You can make words disappear."

For `display: none;` you'll get
"This is just like . You can make words disappear."

Exercise 6

Download the source code for this exercise from
http://learncodingfast.com/css and unzip the file. The
source code for this exercise can be found in the *Chapter 6
- Display and Visibility* folder.

Exercise 6.1

1. Open the file *Chapter 6 - Display and Visibility.html*
   concurrently in your browser and text editor.

2. Change the height and width in the CSS declaration for
   `#displaydemo`. Observe what happens to the yellow
   box.

   Nothing changes right? The yellow box is declared as
   an inline element. Hence it will only take up as much
   width and height as it needs. In fact, you can remove
   the height and width properties and nothing will
   change.

3. Now change the display property of `#displaydemo`
   from `display: inline;` to `display: block;`. What
   happens?

   The yellow box is now displayed as a block element. It

starts and ends with a new line. If you have declared its width and height, the width and height will be the values you specified. If you have not specified its width and height, the yellow box will occupy the full width of the page. It will take up as much height as it needs.

4. Try changing the height and width in the CSS declaration for `#displaydemo`. Observe what happens.

5. Now, let's move on to the `visibility` property. Change the CSS declaration of `#magic` from `display: inline;` to `visibility: hidden;`. Observe what happens to the word 'magic' in the blue sentence.

6. Next, change the CSS declaration of #magic from `visibility: hidden;` to `display: none;`. Observe what happens.

Chapter 7: Background

In this chapter, we'll learn how to change the background properties of an element. These properties include changing its background color and background image.

For a start, let us first look at how to change the background color.

Background Color

To declare the background color of an element, we use the `background-color` property. Similar to how we specify the border color of our CSS boxes, we can declare the background color of an element using one of three notations: color name, rgb notation or hexadecimal notation.

Examples:

```
background-color: green;
background-color: rgb(0, 255, 0);
background-color: #00FF00;
```

Background Image

If you find it plain to just use color as the background of an element, you can choose to use an image. CSS allows us great flexibility in how we want the image to be displayed.

background-image

To use an image as the background, we specify the URL to the image using the `background-image` property.

Example:

```
background-image: url("image1.jpg");
```

background-repeat

By default, the background image is placed at the top-left corner of the element, and repeated both vertically and horizontally. If you do not want the background image to be repeated, you can use the `background-repeat` property to change it. The following list shows some commonly used values for the `background-repeat` property:

`repeat`
This is the default. Image will be repeated horizontally and vertically.

`repeat-x`
Image will only be repeated horizontally.

`repeat-y`
Image will only be repeated vertically.

`no-repeat`
Image will not be repeated.

Example:

```
background-repeat: repeat-x;
```

background-attachment

The `background-attachment` property specifies whether the background image should be fixed or scroll with the page. The two commonly used values are `fixed` and `scroll`. The default is `scroll`. Try the exercise at the end of this chapter to see how this works.

Example:

```
background-attachment: scroll;
```

background-position

The `background-position` property is very useful if you want to specify which area of the background image you want to display.

Suppose you have an element with width and height 100px each. If the background image that you use has width 200px and height 300px, only a portion of the background image will be displayed as the image is larger than the size of the element.

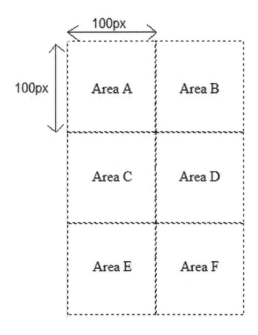

For instance, if you use the image above (200px by 300px) as the background image of a 100px by 100px element, only Area A (top left) will be displayed by default. What if you want to display Area F instead? To do that, you need to change the value of the `background-position` property.

The most common way to specify the `background-position` value is to use pixels. The syntax is:

```
background-position: xpos ypos;
```

To understand how this syntax works, let's imagine a piece of cardboard with a 100px by 100px hole in the middle. This hole in the cardboard represents the HTML element. Now imagine your background image is underneath that cardboard. By default, the image will be aligned such that

Area A is shown through the hole in the cardboard. If you want to display Area F instead, you have to shift the image (not the cardboard) 100px to the left and 200px up. To achieve this with CSS, you write:

```
background-position: -100px -200px;
```

The first number (-100px) shifts the image horizontally. If this number is positive, the image is shifted to the right. If negative, it is shifted to the left.

The second number (-200px) shifts the image vertically. If this number is positive, the image is shifted down. If negative, it is shifted up.

The best way to understand this concept is to try the exercises for this Chapter. I strongly encourage you to do them before moving on to Chapter 8.

Exercise 7

Download the source code for this exercise from http://learncodingfast.com/css and unzip the file. The source code for this exercise can be found in the *Chapter 7 - Background* folder.

Exercise 7.1

1. Open the file *Chapter 7 - Background.html* concurrently in your browser and text editor.

2. Scroll the page in your browser window. The *Learn Coding Fast* logo is set as the background for the `body` element. Notice what happens to the logo as you scroll.

   Now in the CSS declaration for `body`, change `background-attachment: fixed;` to `background-attachment: scroll;`. Refresh and scroll the page. Notice what happens.

3. Next, change `background-repeat: repeat-x;` in the `body` CSS rules to each of the following and notice what happens to the background logo.

   (a) `background-repeat: repeat;`
   (b) `background-repeat: no-repeat;`
   (c) `background-repeat: repeat-y;`

   Notice what happens in each case.

4. Next, change `background-color: white;` to `background-color: #0000FF;`. This should change the background color of the page to blue.

5. Finally, we are going to look at the `background-position` property. We'll be modifying the rules for `#box1` in the examples that follow. The image used in this example is 'backgroundposition.png' stored in the same folder. Have a look at the image before proceeding.

   Notice that when `background-position` is set to `0 0`

(the default), area A is displayed. Changing the `background-position` property will shift the background image with reference to area A.

In the source code CSS declaration for `#box1`, change `background-position: 0 0;` to

(a) `background-position: -100px 0;`
This shifts the background image 100px to the left. As the default area shown is Area A, after shifting 100px to the left, you should get Area B.

(b) `background-position: 100px 0;`
This shifts the background image 100px to the right. As the `background-repeat` property is set to `no-repeat`, no image will be displayed. This is because the background image has shifted out of the boundaries of `box1`.

(c) `background-position: 0 -100px;`
This shifts the background image 100px up. You should get Area C.

(d) `background-position: 0 100px;`
This shifts the background image 100px down. No image will be displayed as the background image has shifted out of the boundaries of `box1`.

(e) `background-position: -100px -100px;`
Try to figure out which area you'll get.

Chapter 8: Text and Font

Text and font properties in CSS are used to format the appearance of words and text on a webpage. The `font` property is concerned with how the characters look, such as whether they are 'fat' or 'thin', 'big' or 'small', and what font type to use. The `text` property is used to style everything else. In this chapter, we'll be covering the `text` and `font` properties commonly used.

Font Properties

font-family

The `font-family` property is used to set the font type.

There are three main categories of font types: serif, san serif and monospace.

Serif fonts have a small line at the end of some characters. Examples include "Times New Roman" and Georgia.

San Serif fonts do not have lines at the end of characters. Examples include Arial and Verdana.

Monospace fonts use the same amount of space for all characters. For instance, the letter 'i' has the same width as the letter 'a'. Examples of monospace fonts include "Courier New" and "Lucida Console".

When specifying the `font-family` property, you should always include several font names so that if the browser does not support the first font, it can try the next font until it finds one that it supports. Start with a more specific font (such as "Times New Roman") and end with a generic font family. If the font name is more than one word, quotation marks should be used.

Example:

```
font-family: "Times New Roman", Times, serif;
```

font-size

The `font-size` property sets the size of the text. Font size can be set with pixels (px), em, percentage (%) or by using keywords.

Using px

The default font size used on most browsers is 16 pixels. If you want your site to display with a different font size, you can specify it like this: `font-size: 20px;`.

Using em

An em is is equal to the current font size. If the element is the child of another element, the current font size is the font size of the parent element. If the element is not a child of any element, the current font size is the browser's default font size. As mentioned above, the default font size used on most browsers is 16px. Hence by default 1em = 16px.

However, this default font size can be changed by changing the browser's setting. For instance, to change the default font size on Firefox, click on the menu button (the right most button with three horizontal lines), select "Options' and finally select the "Content' tab. You can then change the current font size under the 'Fonts & Colors' section.

If the user sets the default font size to 20px, 1em becomes 20px. If you want the font size to be 1.5 times the current font size, you simply write 1.5em. The em is the prefered unit size used by most developers as the default font size can be customised by the user.

Using Percentage

Percentage is similar to em. 200% simply means 2 times the current font size. Hence, 200% = 2em.

Using Keywords

The final way to specify font size is to use keywords. Commonly used keywords are xx-small, x-small, small, medium (this is the default), large, x-large and xx-large.

Examples:

```
font-size: 40px;
font-size: 1.5em;
font-size: 120%;
font-size: large;
```

font-style

The `font-style` property is used to specify italic text. The two common values are `normal` and `italic`. Normal will display text with <u>no</u> italic while italic displays text in italic.

Example:

```
font-style: italic;
```

font-weight

The `font-weight` property is the counterpart of `font-style`. While `font-style` is used to specify italic text, `font-weight` is used to specify bold text. Commonly used values include `normal`, `bold`, `bolder` and `lighter`. Alternatively, you can also specify the thickness of the characters using numbers in multiples of 100, from 100 (thinnest) to 900 (thickest). 400 is the normal thickness, and 700 is the same as bold.

However, note that most web browsers only support `normal` and `bold` font weights. In that case, 100-500 correspond to `normal` while 600 and above correspond to `bold`.

Examples:

```
font-weight: bold;
font-weight: 300;
```

Text Properties

CSS `text` properties allow you to set properties that are not related to the font of the text. Common properties include text color, text alignment, text decoration, letter spacing, word spacing and line height.

color

The CSS `color` property specifies the color of the text. Similar to what we learned in Chapter 4 regarding the `border-color` property, text color can be specified in one of three ways: using a color name, a RGB value or a hex value.

Examples:

```
color: blue;
color: #00ff00;
color: rgb(255,0,0);
```

text-alignment

The `text-alignment` property allows us to specify whether we want text to be centered, or aligned to the left or right, or justified. The commonly used values are `left`, `right`, `center` and `justify`.

Example:

```
text-align: center;
```

text-decoration

The `text-decoration` property is mainly used to specify whether the text should be decorated with a line. The commonly used values are `none` (i.e. just normal text, no decoration), `underline`, `overline` (a line above the text) and `line-through` (a line through the text).

This property is commonly used to remove underlines from hyperlinks. By default, most browsers will display hyperlinks in blue, with an underline. You can use the code `text-decoration: none;` to remove the underline.

Example:

```
text-decoration: none;
```

letter-spacing

Letter spacing is used to increase or decrease the spacing between letters in a word. You specify the amount of spacing in pixels. To increase the spacing, use a positive value. To decrease it, use a negative value.

For instance, `letter-spacing: 2px;` will cause the letters to be spaced 2 pixels apart. `letter-spacing: -1px;` will cause the letters to be cramped together, overlapping each other by 1 pixel.

Example:

```
letter-spacing: 2px;
```

word-spacing

Word spacing, on the other hand, is used to increase or decrease the spacing between words in text. Similar to `letter-spacing`, you specify the amount of spacing in pixels, using positive to increase the spacing and negative to decrease it.

Example:

```
word-spacing: 2px;
```

line-height

Line height is used to set the spacing between each line of text. This property can be set using a number, a specific length, or a percentage.

When using a number to specify `line-height`, the given number will be multiplied with the current font size to give the line height. For instance, `line-height: 2` will result in a line height of 32px if the current font size is 16px.

When using length to specify `line-height`, units such as px (pixel), em, cm, pt (point, where 1 point = 1/72 of 1in) etc can be used.

When using percentage, the given percentage will be multiplied with the current font size to give the line height. For instance, `line-height: 50%` will result in a line-height of 8px if the current font size is 16px. Note that `line-height` does not alter the font size. A line height of 8px will result in the lines overlapping each other.

Examples:

```
line-height: 20px;
line-height: 120%;
```

To have a better understanding of how each of these properties work, try the exercise below.

Exercise 8

Download the source code for this exercise from http://learncodingfast.com/css and unzip the file. The source code for this exercise can be found in the *Chapter 8 - Font and Text* folder.

Exercise 8.1

1. Open the file *Chapter 8 - Font and Text.html* concurrently in your browser and text editor.

2. Modify the CSS property `font-family` and observe what happens to the sample text. The current font family is Sans Serif. Try each of the following:

(a) `font-family: Verdana, Arial, Helvetica, sans-serif;`

(b) `font-family: Courier, "Lucida Console", monospace;`

3. Modify the CSS property `font-size` and observe what happens to the sample text in each of the following cases. Try

   (a) `font-size: 40px;`
   (b) `font-size: 1.5em;`
   (c) `font-size: x-small;`
   (d) `font-size: 120%;`

4. Modify the CSS property `font-style` and observe what happens to the sample text. Try

   (a) `font-style: italic;`

5. Modify the CSS property `font-weight` and observe what happens to the sample text. Try

   (a) `font-weight: bold;`
   (b) `font-weight: 300;`

6. Modify the CSS property `color` and observe what happens to the sample text. Try

   (a) `color: blue;`
   (b) `color: #00ff00;`

(c) `color: rgb(255,0,0);`

7. Modify the CSS property `text-align` and observe what happens to the sample text. By default, the text in this paragraph is left aligned. Now try each of the following:

   (a) `text-align: justify;`
   (b) `text-align: right;`
   (c) `text-align: center;`

8. Modify the CSS property `text-decoration` and observe what happens to the sample text. Try

   (a) `text-decoration: underline;`
   (b) `text-decoration: overline;`
   (c) `text-decoration: line-through;`

9. Modify the CSS property `letter-spacing` and observe what happens to the sample text. Try

   (a) `letter-spacing: 5px;`
   (b) `letter-spacing: -5px;`

10. Change `letter-spacing` back to `0px`. Modify the CSS property `word-spacing` and observe what happens to the sample text. Try

    (a) `word-spacing: 10px;`
    (b) `word-spacing: -20px;`

11. Change `word-spacing` back to `0px`. Modify the CSS property `line-height` and observe what happens to the sample text. Try

(a) `line-height: 2;`
(b) `line-height: 25px;`
(c) `line-height: 30%;`

Chapter 9: Lists, Links and Navigation Bars

In this chapter, we'll be looking at CSS properties for styling hyperlinks and lists. In addition, we'll combine both concepts and discuss how to create navigation bars commonly seen on web pages. Ready? Let's first start with CSS list.

CSS Lists

Recall that in HTML, we can create two different types of list: ordered list and unordered list? We can style these lists using CSS list properties.

list-style-type

The `list-style-type` property allows you to set list item markers for your lists. List item markers refer to those bullets/numbers/letters on the left of each list item.

For ordered lists, we can specify the type of numbers or letters we want to use as markers. For instance, if we want to use roman numbers (e.g. i, ii, iii) as item markers, we can write `list-style-type: lower-roman;`.

Other commonly used markers include:

`decimal` (this is the default),

`decimal-leading-zero` (number with a leading zero, e.g. 01, 02..),
`lower-alpha` (e.g. a, b, c..),
`lower-greek` (e.g. α, β, γ..),
`upper-alpha` (e.g. A, B, C..) and
`upper-roman` (e.g. I, II, III…).

For unordered list, you can specify the shape that you want to use as the bullet. The default marker is a `disc` (a filled circle). You can change that to either a `square` or a `circle`.

In addition, you can also choose not to use any item marker for your list. To do that, you write `list-style-type: none;`. This is commonly done when creating navigation bars.

Examples:

```
list-style-type: lower-roman;
list-style-type: circle;
list-style-type: none;
```

list-style-image

If you do not fancy any of the provided list styles, you can choose to use an image as the list item marker. To do that, you use the `list-style-image` property to specify the url of the image to use.

Examples:

```
list-style-image: url('myMarker.gif');
```

list-style-position

The `list-style-position` property is used to specify whether the list item markers should appear inside or outside the content flow. There are two acceptable values: `inside` and `outside`.

By default, list items are displayed with a certain amount of indentation. If `list-style-position` is set to `inside`, the list item markers are displayed after the indentation. The indentation is represented by the left edge of the boxes in the image below. If `list-style-position` is set to `outside`, the markers are displayed before the indentation.

Inside:

Outside:

In other words, `list-style-position: inside` will result in more indentation than `list-style-position: outside`. The default position is `outside`.

Examples:

```
list-style-position: outside;
```

list-style

`list-style` is a shorthand property for setting all the list properties (i.e. `list-style-type`, `list-style-position` and `list-style-image`) in one declaration. If any value is missing, the default value for the missing property will be used.

Examples:

```
list-style: square inside url("myMarker.gif");
```

CSS Links

Hyperlinks can be styled using any of the CSS properties discussed in previous chapters. You can style the background color using the `background-color` property. This will give the link a highlighted appearance. You can also use the text and font properties covered in Chapter 8 to change the font size, font style, text color, text decoration etc.

In addition, we can choose to style hyperlinks based on the state they are in. Links can be in one of four states:

link (an unvisited link)
visited (a visited link)
hover (when the user mouses over it), or
active (when the link is clicked).

To specify the state, we write a:link, a:visited, a:hover or a:active. You should always specify the 4 states in the order above.

Examples:

```
a {
      text-decoration: none;
}

a:link {
      color: #0000FF;
}

a:visited {
      color: #00FF00;
}

a:hover {
      color: #FFFF00;
}

a:active {
      color: #FF00FF;
}
```

Navigation Bars

Navigation bars are commonly created as an unordered list in HTML and styled using list and link properties in CSS.

Let's try creating our own navigation bar. First, we need to create an unordered list of items for our menu and make the list items clickable (as hyperlinks).

```
<ul>
      <li><a href="home.html">Home</a></li>
      <li><a href="htmltutorial.html">HTML
Tutorial</a></li>
      <li><a href="csstutorial.html">CSS
Tutorial</a></li>
      <li><a
href="javascripttutorial.html">Javascript
Tutorial</a></li>
</ul>
```

Next, let's add the following declaration to our CSS style to remove the default bullet from the list.

```
ul {
      list-style-type: none;
}
```

Now, we have to style the hyperlinks. We'll use a block display which allows us to specify the width of the links. In addition, we'll center align the text and remove all underlines. We'll also add a background color to our links.

```
a {
      display: block;
```

```
       width: 160px;
       text-align: center;
       text-decoration: none;
       background-color: #00FF00;
}
```

Finally, if we want the navigation bar to be a horizontal bar, we need to float the list items left. Otherwise, the list items will be displayed as a vertical bar.

```
li {
       float: left;
}
```

There you go! We've just created a simple horizontal navigation bar. The source code for this navigation bar is given as part of the exercise for this chapter. Play around with it and try to make it more visually appealing. You can also specify different styles for the four different link states.

This method is just one of the methods to create a navigation bar. The accompanying project for this book will demonstrate a different method.

Exercise 9

Download the source code for this exercise from http://learncodingfast.com/css and unzip the file. The source code for this exercise can be found in the *Chapter 9 - Lists, Links and Navigation Bars* folder.

Exercise 9.1

1. Open the file *Chapter 9 - List and Links.html* concurrently in your browser and text editor.

2. Modify the CSS declaration for `ol` and observe what happens to the 'Cars Ordered List'. Try each of the following:

    (a) `list-style-type: decimal-leading-zero;`
    (b) `list-style-type: lower-roman;`
    (c) `list-style-type: upper-roman;`
    (d) `list-style-type: upper-alpha;`
    (e) `list-style-type: lower-alpha;`
    (f) `list-style-type: lower-greek;`
    (g) `list-style-type: none;`

3. Modify the CSS declaration for `ul` and observe what happens to the 'Cars Unordered List'. Try each of the following:

    (a) `list-style-type: circle;`
    (b) `list-style-type: square;`
    (c) `list-style-type: none;`
    (d) `list-style-type: disc;`

4. Add the following rule to the CSS declaration for `ul`:

    `list-style-position: outside;`

    Refresh the browser. Nothing changes right? That is

because `list-style-position: outside;` is the default. Now change `list-style-position: outside;` to `list-style-position: inside;`. You'll notice that the unordered list is shifted slightly to the right (i.e. there's more indentation).

5. Remove the `list-style-type` property for `ul` and add the following instead:

   (a) `list-style-image: url("myMarker.gif");`

   Observe what happens to the 'Cars Unordered List'.

6. Now let's look at how to style hyperlinks. Try adding the following rules to the stated selector:

   (a) Add `color: green;` to `a:link{}` and observe what happens to the 'Click Me' link.

   (b) Add `font-size: 2em;` to `a:active{}` and click on the link.

   (c) Add `background-color: red;` to `a:hover{}` and hover your mouse over the link.

Exercise 9.2

1. Open the file *Chapter 9 - Navigation Bar.html* concurrently in your browser and text editor.

2. This page shows an example of how a horizontal navigation bar can be created using CSS rules for lists and links. The steps are explained in the book. Study the code and try modifying the CSS declaration to improve the design of this navigation bar.

Chapter 10: Tables

HTML tables are ugly looking by default. However, with some simple CSS styling, we can easily convert them into gorgeous looking tables. In this chapter, we'll look at how to do that.

Border, Padding and Margin

The first set of properties we'll be looking at is the `border`, `padding` and `margin` properties. Recall we talked about these properties when discussing the CSS box model? HTML tables (`<table>`) and table cells (`<th>` and `<td>`) follow the same box model as other CSS elements and can therefore be styled using these properties.

Table Margin

Table Padding		
Firstname	**Lastname**	**Age**
Derek	Lee	24
Aaron	Flynn	16
Joe	Murphy	31

To understand how this work, refer to the diagram on the previous page (the words 'Table Margin' and 'Table Padding' are added for reference and do not exist on the actual table).

The CSS rules for this table are as follows:

```
table {
      border: dashed 1px black;
      padding: 50px;
      margin: 60px;
}

th {
      border: solid 1px black;
      padding: 30px;
      text-align: center;
}

td {
      border: solid 1px black;
      padding: 20px;
}
```

The dotted line is the table's border. Space surrounding the dotted border is the table's margin (declared to be 60px) and space within the dotted border is its padding (50px).

The first row (Firstname, Lastname, Age) is defined as the table heading using the <th> tag. Space surrounding the words 'Firstname', 'Lastname' and 'Age' is the padding for the <th> element (30px).

The second, third and fourth row is defined using the <td> tag. Space surrounding words like 'Derek', 'Aaron' and '31' is the padding for the <td> element (20px).

No margins are declared for the <th> and <td> elements as margins are ignored for table cells. Hence, we cannot specify the spacing between the cells. By default, there'll be a small gap between individual table cells. In addition, there's also a gap between the table's border (the dotted line) and the borders of the cells (the solid lines) even if you set table padding to 0px. If you only want one border, you have to use the border-collapse property:

```
border-collapse: collapse;
```

We'll have a chance to play around with the border, padding and margin properties when we do the exercise for this chapter. For now, let's move on to the next property.

Height and Width

The width and height of a table can be set using the width and height properties. The values are normally given in pixels or as a percentage. For instance, the code below sets the table width to be 100% of the parent element and the height to be 500px.

```
table {
        width: 100%;
        height: 500px;
```

```
}
```

You can also use the height property at the `tr`, `th` or `td`
level. For instance, if you want the table header row to have
a height of 100px, you can write

```
th {
        height: 100px;
}
```

In addition, you can set the width property at the table cell
level (i.e. for the `td` and `th` elements). If you want the table
cells to have a width of 200px, you can write

```
th {
        width: 200px;
}
```

If you want to style individual columns, you can use the
`id`/`class` attribute to do it. For instance if you have the
table structure below:

```
<table>
        <tr>
                <th id="firstColumn">First
        Column</th>
                <th id="secondColumn">First
Column</th>
        </tr>
        <tr>
                <td>Some data</th>
                <td>More data</th>
        </tr>
</table>
```

you can set the width of the table columns individually like this:

```
#firstColumn {
       width: 40%;
}

#secondColumn {
       width: 60%;
}
```

Text Alignment

Text within table cells can be aligned horizontally using the text-align property and vertically using the vertical-align property. The commonly used values for the text-align property are center, left, right and justify. The commonly used values for the vertical-align property are top, middle and bottom.

Examples:

```
th {
       text-align: center;
       vertical-align: middle;
}
```

Background, Font and Text

Tables can also be styled using properties for background, font and text covered in Chapter 7 and 8. For instance, the code below will set the text color of `<th>` elements to white and give the elements a green background color.

```
th {
    background-color: green;
    color: white;
}
```

nth-child( ) Selector

Sometimes when we have a very large table with a lot of rows, the table may be difficult to read.
One way to improve the readability of large tables is to color alternating rows. This can be easily achieved with the `nth-child( )` selector.

To color even rows, we write

```
tr:nth-child(even) {
    background-color: lightgreen;
}
```

To color odd rows, we write

```
tr:nth-child(odd) {
    background-color: lightgray;
}
```

Exercise 10

Download the source code for this exercise from http://learncodingfast.com/css and unzip the file. The source code for this exercise can be found in the *Chapter 10 - Tables* folder.

Exercise 10.1

1. Open the file *Chapter 10 - Tables.html* concurrently in your browser and text editor.

2. Modify the CSS declaration for `table` and observe what happens to the table. Try adding the following and observe what happens in each case:

   (a) `padding: 50px;`
   (b) `margin: 30px;`
   (c) `border-collapse: collapse;`
   (d) Change `border: dashed 1px black;` to `border: solid 2px green;`

3. Modify the CSS declaration for `th` and observe what happens to the table. Try adding:

   (a) `padding: 50px;`
   (b) `margin: 30px;` (Margin rules will be ignored. Try it)

   Repeat the same for `td`.

4. Remove the `padding` and `margin` properties from Part 3 for both `td` and `th`. Modify the CSS declaration for `table` and observe what happens to the table. Try adding each of the following:

(a) `width: 300px;`

(b) `width: 50%;`
Notice that the width of the table is now 50% of the red box.

(c) `height: 500px;`

(d) `height: 80%;`
Notice that the height of the table is now 80% of the red box.

5. Remove the `height` and `width` properties for `table` from Part 4. Modify the CSS declaration for <u>th</u> and observe what happens to the table. Try changing the `height` property to:

(a) `height: 100px;`

Remove the `height` property from `th` and add it to `td`. Notice what happens. Repeat the same for `tr`.

6. Modify the CSS declaration for `th` and observe what happens to the table. Try changing the `width` property to:

(a) `width: 100px;`

Remove the `width` property from `th` and add it to `td`. Notice what happens. There should be no difference as whether you set the width of a table cell at the `th` or `td` level, that width will affect both elements.

7. Add the attributes `id="firstColumn"`, `id="secondColumn"` and `id="thirdColumn"` to the first, second and third `<th>` start tags respectively. Next, add the following CSS rules to adjust the width of the three columns separately:

```
#firstColumn {
    width: 100px;
}
#secondColumn {
    width: 200px;
}
#thirdColumn {
    width: 50px;
}
```

Refresh the page and observe what happens. Try adjusting the width with different values.

8. Modify the CSS declaration for `tr` and observe what happens to the table. Try adding:

   (a) `text-align: center;`
   (b) `vertical-align: top;`

   Remove the above properties from `tr` and add them to `th`. Notice what happens. Repeat the same for `td`. If you do not see any difference, try increasing the width of the table and/or the height of the rows.

9. Modify the CSS declaration for `tr` and observe what happens to the table. Try adding:

(a) `background-color: green;`

(b) `color: white;`

Remove the above properties from `tr` and add them to `th`. Notice what happens.

Now, remove the properties from `th` and add them to `td`.

10. Finally, let's try coloring alternating rows. Remove the `background-color` and `color` rules from `td` first. Next, add the following code and observe what happens.

```css
tr:nth-child(even) {
    background-color: lightgreen;
}

tr:nth-child(odd) {
    background-color: lightgray;
}
```

Bonus Project

Congratulations! We've now covered enough fundamentals of CSS (and HTML) to start coding our first webpage from scratch. The best way to learn CSS is by doing. Hence, I've included a bonus project with this book where you'll be guided through the coding of a webpage for a fictitious travel agency. You can check out the demo for the project at http://www.learncodingfast.com/demo/jetspeed.html.

The bonus project can be downloaded at http://learncodingfast.com/css.

I strongly encourage you to try the project as it'll give you a chance to see how all the concepts that you've learnt in this book tie together. Working through the project will help solidify your learning and fill all the gaps that you may have.

Have fun coding!

Thank You

We've come to the end of the book. Thank you for reading this book and I hope you have enjoyed the book. More importantly, I sincerely hope the book has helped you master the fundamentals of CSS.

I know you could have picked from a dozen of books on CSS, but you took a chance with this book. Thank you once again for downloading this book and reading all the way to the end. Please try the exercises and the bonus project. You'll learn a lot by doing.

Now I'd like to ask for a "small" favor. Could you please take a minute or two to leave a review for this book on Amazon?

This feedback will help me tremendously and will help me continue to write more guides on programming. If you like the book or have any suggestions for improvement, please let me know. I will be deeply grateful. :)

Last but not least, remember you can download the bonus project and the source code for the exercises at http://www.learncodingfast.com/css.

You can also contact me at jamie@learncodingfast.com.

Appendix A: Source Code for Exercises

Exercise 3.1

```
<!doctype html>
<html>
<head><title>Chapter 3 - Basics of CSS</title>
<style>
p{
        background-color: yellow;
}
</style>
</head>
<body>
<h1>Chapter 3 - Basics of CSS</h1>
<h2>CSS Selectors</h2>

<p>This exercise uses background color to help us figure
out which element we are selecting. This paragraph has no
class or id.</p>

<p id = "myIDPara">This paragraph has id =
"myIDPara".</p>

<p class = "myClassPara">This paragraph has class =
"myClassPara".</p>
```

```
<p class = "myClassPara mySecondClassPara">This
paragraph has class = "myClassPara" and class =
"mySecondClassPara".</p>

<div>
        This is some text in the div element.

        <p>This paragraph is the first child element of the
'div' element.</p>
        <p>This paragraph is the second child element of
the 'div' element.</p>
        <p>This paragraph is the third child element of the
'div' element.</p>
</div>

<a href="http://www.learncodingfast.com">Learn Coding
Fast</a><br>
<a href="http://www.google.com">Google</a>

</body></html>
```

Exercise 4.1

```
<!doctype html>
<html>
<head><title>Chapter 4 - CSS Box Model</title>
<style type="text/css">
#box1 {
        margin: 20px;
        padding: 10px;
        border: 5px solid black;
        width: 100px;
        height: 100px;
        text-align: justify;
        float: left;
}
#box2 {
        margin: 20px;
        padding: 50px;
        border: 5px solid black;
        width: 100px;
        height: 100px;
        text-align: justify;
        float: left;
}
</style></head>
<body>

<div id="box1">Learn CSS in One Day and Learn It Well.
CSS is easy.</div>
<div id="box2">Learn CSS in One Day and Learn It Well.
CSS is easy.</div>
```

<p>skajd fhadlc vkas j cnl ka jshvn aclaks jdclkasjd ckasj cnkas djvcn ksa mc nlkasd jn skajd fhadlc vkas j cnl ka jshvn aclaks jdclkasjd ckasj cnkas djvcn ksa mc nlkasd jn skajd fhadlc vkas j cnl ka jshvn aclaks jdclkasjd ckasj cnkas djvcn ksa mc nlkasd jn</p>
</body></html>

Exercise 5.1

```
<!DOCTYPE html>
<html>
<head><title>Chapter 5 - Positioning</title>
<style type="text/css">
#box1 {
        background-color: green;
        width: 100px;
        height: 100px;
        padding: 10px;
        border: 5px solid black;
        margin: 20px;
}
#box2 {
        background-color: red;
        width: 50px;
        height: 50px;
        padding: 20px;
        border: 5px dotted black;
        margin: 10px;
}
p {
}
</style></head>
<body>
        <div id="box1"></div>
        <div id="box2"></div>
        <p>This is some text added to demonstrate the
concept of overlapping.</p>
</body></html>
```

Exercise 5.2

```
<!doctype html>
<html>
<head><title>Chapter 5 - Floating</title>
<style type="text/css">
div {
        padding: 10px;
        border: 1px dashed black;
        margin: 5px;
        float: left;
}
#box1 {
        width: 60px;
        height: 100px;
}
#box2 {
        width: 100px;
        height: 20px;
}
#box3 {
        width: 50px;
        height: 150px;
}
#box4 {
        width: 20px;
        height: 50px;
}
#box5 {
        width: 150px;
        height: 120px;
}
#box6 {
        width: 120px;
```

```
        height: 70px;
}
#box7 {
        width: 25px;
        height: 80px;
}
</style></head>

<body>
        <div id="box1">Box 1</div>
        <div id="box2">Box 2</div>
        <div id="box3">Box 3</div>
        <div id="box4">Box 4</div>
        <div id="box5">Box 5</div>
        <div id="box6">Box 6</div>
        <div id="box7">Box 7</div>
 </body></html>
```

Exercise 6.1

```
<!doctype html>
<html>
<head><title>Chapter 6 - Display and Visibility</title>
<style type="text/css">

#displaydemo {
        border: 1px dashed black;
        background-color: yellow;
        display: inline;
        width: 100px;
        height: 100px;
}

#magic {
        display: inline;
}

#magicsentence {
        color: blue;
        font-size: 2em;
}
</style></head>

<body>
        <p>This <span id="displaydemo">yellow box</span> is
used to demonstrate the difference between an inline and a
block element.</p>
        <p id="magicsentence">"This is just like <span
id="magic">magic</span>. You can make words
disappear."</p>
</body></html>
```

Exercise 7.1

```
<!doctype html>
<html>
<head><title>Chapter 7 - Background</title>
<style type="text/css">

body {
        background-color: white;
        background-image: url("learncodingfast.png");
        background-repeat: repeat-x;
        background-attachment: fixed;
}

#box1 {
        width: 100px;
        height: 100px;
        background-repeat: no-repeat;
        background-color: blue;
        background-image: url("backgroundposition.png");
        background-position: 0 0;
}

#box2 {
        height: 1000px;
}
</style>
</head>
<body>
        <div id="box1"></div>
        <div id="box2"></div>
</body></html>
```

Exercise 8.1

```html
<!doctype html>
<html>
<head>
<title>Chapter 8 - Font and Text</title>

<style type="text/css">

#sampletext{
        width: 300px;
        border: 1px solid black;
        padding: 20px;
        font-family: Times, "Times New Roman", Georgia, serif;
        font-size: 1em;
        font-style: normal;
        font-weight: normal;
        color: black;
        text-align: left;
        text-decoration: none;
        letter-spacing: 0px;
        word-spacing: 0px;
        line-height: 1;
}

</style>
</head>
<body>
        <h3>Sample Text</h3>
        <p id="sampletext">This paragraph of text is used
```

to demonstrate the effects of various font and text
properties. Modify the CSS declaration for "sampletext"
and observe what happens to this paragraph of text. A

border is given to this paragraph of text in order to show the effect of 'justify'.</p>
</body></html>

Exercise 9.1

```
<!doctype html>
<html>
<head>
<title>Chapter 9 - Lists and Links</title>

<style type="text/css">

body { padding-left: 20px; }
div { font-weight: bold; text-decoration: underline; font-size: 1.2em; padding-top: 5px;}
ol {
        list-style-type: decimal;
}
ul {
        list-style-type: disc;
}
a { text-decoration: none;}
a:link { }
a:visited { }
a:hover { }
a:active { }
</style>

</head>
<body>
<div>Styling HTML Lists</div>
<p>This section is to demonstrate how you can style ordered and unordered lists in CSS</p>
Cars Ordered List
<ol>
```

```
        <li>Ford</li>
        <li>Honda</li>
        <li>Toyota</li>
</ol>
Cars Unordered List
<ul>
        <li>Ford</li>
        <li>Honda</li>
        <li>Toyota</li>
</ul>
<hr>
<div>Styling Hyperlinks</div>
<p>This section is to demonstrate how you can style
hyperlinks in CSS</p>
<a href="somepage.html">Click Me</a>
</body>
</html>
```

Exercise 9.2

```
<!DOCTYPE html>
<html>
<head><title>Chapter 9 - Navigation Bar</title>
<style>
ul {
        list-style-type: none;
}

a {
        display: block;
        width: 160px;
        text-align: center;
```

```
        text-decoration: none;
        background-color: #00FF00;
}

li {
        float: left;
}
</style>
</head>
<body>
<ul>
        <li><a href="home.html">Home</a></li>
        <li><a href="htmltutorial.html">HTML Tutorial</a></li>
        <li><a href="csstutorial.html">CSS Tutorial</a></li>
        <li><a href="javascripttutorial.html">Javascript
Tutorial</a></li>
</ul>
</body>
</html>
```

Exercise 10.1

```
<!DOCTYPE html>
<html>
<head><title>Chapter 10 - Tables</title>
<style>
div {
        width: 100%;
        height: 600px;
        border: red solid 1px;
}

table {
        border: dashed 1px black;
}

th {
        border: solid 1px black;
}

td {
        border: solid 1px black;
}

tr {
}
</style>
</head>
<body>
```
The table below is a child element of the red box. The red box is added to show the effects of the height and width properties for 'table'.


```html
<div>
<table>
    <tr><th>Firstname</th><th>Lastname</th>
    <th>Age</th></tr>
    <tr><td>Derek</td><td>Lee</td><td>24</td></tr>
    <tr><td>Aaron</td><td>Flynn</td>
    <td>16</td></tr>
    <tr><td>Joe</td><td>Murphy</td>
    <td>31</td></tr>
</table>
</div>
</body>
</html>
```

Printed in Great Britain
by Amazon